D0778515

ARTISTS OF THE HARLEM RENAISSANCE

LANGSTON HUGHES

REBECCA CAREY ROHAN

Cavendish
Square

New York

Published in 2017 by Cavendish Square Publishing, LLC
243 5th Avenue, Suite 136, New York, NY 10016

Copyright © 2017 by Cavendish Square Publishing, LLC

First Edition

Website: cavendishsq.com

This publication represents the opinions and views of the author based on his or her personal experience, knowledge, and research. The information in this book serves as a general guide only. The author and publisher have used their best efforts in preparing this book and disclaim liability rising directly or indirectly from the use and application of this book.

CPSIA Compliance Information: Batch #CS16CSQ

All websites were available and accurate when this book was sent to press.

Library of Congress Cataloging-in-Publication Data

Names: Rohan, Rebecca Carey, 1967- author.
Title: Langston Hughes : poet / Rebecca Rohan.
Description: New York : Cavendish Square Publishing, 2016.
Series: Artists of the Harlem Renaissance | Includes bibliographical references and index.
Identifiers: LCCN 2015035463 | ISBN 9781502610645 (library bound)
ISBN 9781502610652 (ebook)
Subjects: LCSH: Hughes, Langston, 1902-1967–Juvenile literature.
Poets, American–20th century–Biography–Juvenile literature.
African American poets–Biography–Juvenile literature.
Classification: LCC PS3515.U274 Z6985 2016 | DDC 818/.5209–dc23
LC record available at http://lccn.loc.gov/2015035463

Editorial Director: David McNamara
Editor: Amy Hayes/Elizabeth Schmermund
Copy Editor: Nathan Heidelberger
Art Director: Jeffrey Talbot
Designer: Stephanie Flecha
Production Assistant: Karol Szymczuk
Photo Research: J8 Media

The photographs in this book are used by permission and through the courtesy of:
Robert W. Kelley/The LIFE Picture Collection/Getty Images, cover; Granamour Weems Collection/Alamy Stock Photo, 5; Carl Van Vechten/Library of Congress, 6, 42, 49; Hulton Archive/Getty Images, 10 (used throughout); Courtesy of the Ohio History Connecton, 12; AP Images, 14; Yale Collection of American Literature, Beninecke Rare Book and Manuscript Library/File:Hughes high school 1919 or 1920.jpg/Wikimedia Commons, 17; John Archibald Motley/Library of Congress, 20; H. Curtis Brown (cover image); Du Bois and Dill Publishers (magazine cover)/File:The Brownies' Book, June 1921 cover.jpg/Wikipedia, 24; DanTD/File:135th Street Lenox Ave NE Subway Staircase.JPG/Wikimedia Commons, 26; Mcmillin24/File:NYPL Former 135th Street Branch, Manhattan.jpg/Wikimedia Commons, 28; Detroit Publishing Co./Library of Congress/File:Low Library.jpg/Wikimedia Commons, 31; WEB DuBois, Oswald G. Villard, J. Max Barber, Charles Edward Russell, Kelly Miller, W. S. Braithwaite, M D Maclean/Library of Congress/File:The crisis nov1910.jpg/Wikimedia Commons, 36; Underwood Archives/Getty Images, 40; William Gottleib/Library of Congress, 45; Yale Collection of American Literature, Beninecke Rare Book and Manuscripte Library, 46; New York Public Library/ Schomburg Center For Research In Black Culture, Photographs And Prints Division, 48; Afro American Newspapers/Gado/Getty Images, 52; Yale Collection of American Literature, Beninecke Rare Book and Manuscript Library/File:Ways of white folks cover.jpg/Wikimedia Commons, 56; AP Photo/The Daily Journal, Charles J. Olson, 58; Public Domain/File:Whitman at about fifty.jpg/Wikimedia Commons, 63, Julie Alissi/J8 Media, 64, 74, 84; Lesekreis/File:Library Walk 17.JPG/Wikimedia Commons, 66; Robert W. Kelley/The LIFE Picture Collection/Getty Images, 69, 70; John D. Kisch/Separate Cinema Archive/Getty Images, 76; Paulette D. Harris Artistic Director, Paul Robeson Theatre at the African American Cultural Center, 81; MathieuB/File:Montmartre, Paris..jpg/Wikimedia Commons,87; Everett Collection Historical/Alamy Stock Photo, 88; Winold Reiss/Library of Congress/File:Langston Hughes by Winold Reiss cph.3c11612.jpg/Wikimedia Commons, 90; AP Images, 100; Americasroof/File:Langston-hughes-house-20e127.jpg/Wikimedia Commons, 103; Fred Stein/picturealliance/dpa/AP Images, 104; Beyond My Ken/File:2014 Columbia University Morningside Heights campus from west.jpg/Wikimedia Commons, 106; Boris15/Shutterstock.com, 113; Peter Kramer/Getty Images, 114.

Printed in the United States of America

TABLE OF CONTENTS

Part I: The Life of Langston Hughes

Chapter 1   7
A Lonely Beginning

Chapter 2   27
A New Start

Chapter 3   49
A Literary Life

Part II: The Work of Langston Hughes

Chapter 4   71
A Lifetime of Work

Chapter 5   91
An Appreciation

Chapter 6   105
Five Decades of Writing, Generations of Impact

Chronology   116

Hughes's Most Important Works   118

Glossary   120

Further Information   123

Bibliography   125

Index   126

About the Author   128

PART 1

The Life of Langston Hughes

"I have discovered in life that there are ways of getting almost anywhere you want to go, if you really want to go."

—*Langston Hughes*

Opposite: Langston Hughes was on of the most important writers of his generation.

CHAPTER ONE

A LONELY BEGINNING

I f there is one thing you can say about Langston Hughes that he would probably say about himself, it's that he was an outsider. While he has been remembered as an American poet, the "Voice of Harlem," and an important contributor to both the Harlem Renaissance and American literature, he actually led a nomadic existence; he lived in various places in the United States and Europe, especially in his younger years, which informed his work and his perspectives on life.

It would have been hard for Hughes to feel like he fit in his own family, too. His mother, Carolina "Carrie" Langston, came from African, Native American, and French ancestry. Her father, Hughes's grandfather, was a prominent, fierce abolitionist, and therefore Carrie grew up believing in equal rights. However, because she was female, Carrie often felt frustrated by the limitations placed on a nineteenth-century woman's life—with the added constraint of racism. She spent her adult life moving from place to place,

Opposite: Langston Hughes, as photographed by his friend Carl Van Vechten.

trying to find a job and a lifestyle that suited her ambitions, and her son Langston often came second to her plans and dreams.

Hughes's father, James Nathaniel Hughes, also had African and Native American ancestors, along with French and Jewish blood. In modern times, Langston Hughes would be considered mixed race. In the era in which he lived, he was considered black—and while his mother and her family tried to instill in him pride in his race, his father actually despised black people, or rather, his perception of them. To James, being black in America meant poverty and powerlessness, so he left the country, and throughout his son's life, he attempted repeatedly to get him to do the same.

Despite his mother's restlessness, his father's dislike of the United States, and his own travels throughout the world, the Harlem neighborhood in New York City did become the place where Hughes felt most at home. It was the **epicenter** of creativity, nightlife, and expression for African Americans in the 1920s, when he was a young adult. It was where he put down roots of a sort, and where he died. But his story begins in Joplin, Missouri, which, at the time, was not a promising environment for an intelligent young child of color.

When James Langston Hughes was born in Joplin on February 1, 1902, his parents had been married for only a few years, and they had already lost a child. Their relationship was shaky. Additionally, his father, James Nathaniel Hughes, was a deeply unhappy person. **Jim Crow laws** had made life difficult and demeaning for black people in the South. Segregation was rampant. Black people and white people used separate waiting rooms, areas on buses, schools, restaurants, theaters, and water fountains. James was also bitter because he had studied to be a lawyer but was prohibited from taking the **bar exam** because of his color. He believed that an African-American man could not have a good life in the United States, so he decided to leave the country permanently. He moved to Cuba, then to Mexico, where he settled for the rest of his life. Carrie, however, refused to go with him, so Langston Hughes—he was never called James—grew up largely without a father.

By the time Langston was about four or five, James had established himself in the legal and business communities in Mexico City. He was making decent money, and he convinced Carrie to travel there, to see how good their life could be. However, the story goes that shortly after Carrie and Langston arrived, a huge earthquake shook the city, and Carrie was too scared to even consider living there. She left with Langston, and the young boy didn't see his father again for twelve years.

Following their return to the United States, Hughes and his mother moved frequently. In between jaunts to different towns and cities as Carrie tried to find a satisfactory job, they lived with her mother, Mary Langston, in Lawrence, Kansas, smack dab in the middle of the midwestern United States. Mary had a strong influence on Hughes's upbringing in more ways than one.

Mary was already sixty-five years old when Hughes was born, and she had quite a history. She and her first husband, Lewis Sheridan Leary, were active abolitionists, and they served as "conductors" on the Underground Railroad, helping to hide escaped Southern slaves as they made their way to freedom in the North. Then Leary, unbeknownst to Mary, decided to join John Brown's army, a group of radical abolitionists. He participated in their infamous attack on the US **arsenal** at Harpers Ferry, West Virginia, in 1859, and he was killed. The shawl he was wearing at the time, complete with bloodstains and bullet holes, became

HARPER'S FERRY

John Brown was a white, **militant** abolitionist who believed in using violence to end slavery. His intent was to wage war against slavery, and while living in Virginia, he gathered a group of men to seize the federal arsenal at Harpers Ferry (now part of West Virginia). He reasoned that attacking the arsenal was the same as attacking the federal government, and that such an act would send an important message. On October 16, 1859, Brown surrounded himself with an "army" of twenty-one men, one of whom was Lewis Sheridan Leary, Mary Langston's first husband. Together, they launched their attack on the town. They cut telegraph wires, captured the federal armory and arsenal, and took over a business called Hall's Rifle Works, which supplied weapons to the government. They then held sixty residents of the town as hostages, hoping to inspire their hostages' slaves to join their cause. It didn't work. The local militia rushed Brown's "army," and as a result, ten of Brown's men were killed (including both of his sons and Leary), seven were captured, and five escaped. John Brown was arrested for murder, slave insurrection, and treason against the state; he was convicted and hanged for his crimes.

one of Mary's most prized possessions. She would wrap herself in it regularly, and even wrapped Hughes in it when he was young and she was telling him stories. She left the ancient garment to Hughes when she died, and he apparently cherished it.

Mary's second husband, Charles Langston, had also been born free and also actively fought for the rights of African Americans. The illegitimate son of a wealthy white man and his mixed-race housekeeper, Charles was also unusual in that he was allowed to inherit property from his birth father, Ralph Quarles, when Quarles died. He and his brothers left the South and moved to Ohio to escape possible repercussions from that inheritance. Charles's oldest brother, Gideon, became a successful businessman. His younger brother, John, became the first African-American lawyer in Ohio and the first black person to be elected to public office in the United States when he won the position of town clerk of Brownhelm, Ohio, in 1854. John helped to set up the law department at all-black Howard University, became US minister to Haiti at the request of President Rutherford B. Hayes, and finally became a congressman in 1888—the first African American to win a congressional election in the state of Virginia.

Charles was no slouch, either. He graduated from Oberlin College, which is where he met Mary. He gained fame in the abolitionist movement for leading a team to the rescue of an escaped slave, who had been kidnapped by a group of men determined to take him back to the South and return him to his owner. He became active in politics after the Civil War and worked for black suffrage, the right for African Americans to vote, in the state of Kansas. He also edited an African-American newspaper, which was a vehicle to demand equal rights and education. By

Charles Langston, seen here holding his hat to his chest, was a member of the Oberlin Rescuers.

marrying into the prestigious Langston family, Mary became an important part of its history, too.

As for her upbringing, Mary had been born free, had never been a slave, and had even gone to college, which was extremely rare for women of her generation, let alone women of color. In fact, she was the first black woman to graduate from Oberlin College. Between her personal history and her education, she worked to instill a sense of pride in her grandson about his heritage, his family and its history, and about the color of his skin. She told him stories about Frederick Douglass and Sojourner Truth. She took him to see Booker T. Washington speak, and she introduced him to African-American publications like the *Crisis,* the magazine published by the National Association for the Advancement of Colored People (NAACP), which was founded and edited by W. E. B. Du Bois, a prominent black educator and activist. The *Crisis* gave black writers an outlet for both their literature and their social commentaries. When Hughes was eight years old, Mary took him to see President Theodore Roosevelt give a speech in which he paid tribute to Lewis Sheridan Leary and the others who had died during the raid on Harpers Ferry.

THE SCHOOL YEARS BEGIN

One of the first times Hughes and his mother settled down was when he was old enough to start school. Carrie had found a job in Topeka, Kansas, about thirty miles from Lawrence. She enrolled Hughes in an all-white school because the school for African-American children was across town, and apparently, in Topeka at that time, school segregation was not enforced as harshly as it would be many years later. Hughes was very intelligent and a good student, but he faced racism not only from some of his classmates,

Langston Hughes at the age of twelve, in Lawrence, Kansas

but even from some of his teachers. Hughes once said, "all the teachers were nice to me, except one, who sometimes used to make remarks about me being colored. And after such remarks, occasionally the kids would grab stones and tin cans out of the alley and chase me home." However, he also remembered that one white boy always stood up for him, and some of the other children would follow his lead. Hughes decided not to judge all white people by the actions of a few. Looking back as an adult, he said, "I learned early not to hate all white people. And ever since, it has seemed to me that most people are generally good, in every race and every country where I have been."

Hughes and his mother struggled financially, as well. Hughes remembered scrounging for cardboard boxes that they could burn in their stove to keep warm when they couldn't afford wood. However, Carrie also instilled in him a love for theater, taking him whenever possible, and she introduced him to the free wonders of the public library. Hughes once **rhapsodized** about the library in Lawrence: "The silence … the big chairs, and long tables, and the fact that the library was always there and didn't have … any sort of insecurity about it—all made me love it. I believed in books more than people."

By the time Hughes was ready to start second grade, Carrie was ready to move on from their life in Topeka. She asked her mother, Mary, to take him in while she pursued other jobs in various cities. Hughes loved his grandmother, and he continued to do well in school, but he also became very lonely. His grandmother was in her seventies at this point and less active, less inclined to tell stories, and more inclined to sit in silence in her rocking chair. She restricted him from going outside because she was worried about the growing threats of segregation and racial discrimination. He later remembered feeling depressed and left out when he could hear other children outside, playing, while he was forced to sit inside. This is when Hughes found **solace** by reading books and writing poetry. Reading took him away from his sadness, while writing enabled him to let out his feelings in a safe form of expression.

Hughes lived with his grandmother until he was about twelve years old, when she passed away. Through his years with her, Mary had also struggled financially. She owned a large house, and in order to pay the mortgage, she often rented out rooms and sometimes the whole house. When she needed to do that, she and Hughes would go and live with family friends James and Mary Reed. It was the Reeds, whom Hughes referred to as his aunt and uncle, who took Hughes in for two years after Mary died. He loved them, and they loved him, so this was not a hardship. Also, they had steady jobs and a home of their own, so living with them gave Hughes a sense of stability and happiness. Hughes stayed with the Reeds until he was fourteen, when Carrie asked him to come and live with her and her new husband, Homer Clark, and their son, Gwyn, in Lincoln, Illinois. Hughes said good-bye to the Reeds, and Kansas, and went to join his new version of family.

For a time, life was good for the four of them. Hughes liked his stepfather, and after being an only child for so long, he liked having Gwyn around and feeling like they were all a family. Although he was one of only two black children in his class at school, he didn't encounter the blatant racism he had experienced in Kansas. Also, this was the place and time where he first decided that he

Hughes as a high school student in Cleveland, Ohio

might want to be a writer. Toward the end of the school year, his fellow eighth graders anointed him Class Poet. Although in later years he would say that they had probably done so because he was black, and as such was expected to have rhythm, he did write a poem to celebrate their eighth-grade graduation that was met with great praise and applause. "That was the way I began to write poetry," he said.

After that graduation, though, it was time for Hughes to move again. World War I was raging, and with so many white men overseas fighting, job opportunities for black men became plentiful. Homer found a good position at a steel mill in Cleveland, Ohio, so the four of them relocated. Hughes started high school at Central High School, and he excelled at his studies, as always. He was elected to class office, joined different clubs, ran track, and most importantly, he began to find his writing "voice" as he published stories and poems in the school newspaper. In addition to all of these activities, he didn't feel like a minority. There were more children of color, and even kids from other countries. For once, he was not the odd man out.

Then, his sense of stability was shattered yet again. First, his mother separated from Homer Clark, and she and Gwyn moved to Chicago. Hughes spent the summer with them, working a part-time job. His mother tried to convince him to quit school and get a full-time job so he could support the three of them. Hughes wisely decided against this plan. He liked Cleveland, and he liked his school. Luckily for him, his mother reconciled with Clark and returned to Cleveland. Then came a bombshell: his father contacted him for the first time in twelve years and asked him to come down to Mexico City to visit for the summer, if not to live. Hughes was going to have to make some tough decisions. His first one was deciding to travel down to Mexico to see what his father's life was like.

By this time, James Hughes was rich, but he was stingy. Although he had a beautiful house on a large piece of property that included a stable, and a housekeeper and a servant boy to help him keep his household running, he didn't spend money on things like good food. Hughes often found himself eating meals that were no better than what he'd eaten during the lean times with his grandmother and mother. His father also harped on him about continuing to live in the United States and tried to pressure him into a career in accounting. Hughes didn't even like math!

Then there was the matter of James's attitude. Although he himself was black, he was prejudiced against people of color and didn't hide it. Hughes could see why his mother described his father as "as mean and evil a Negro as ever lived." He later described his summer in Mexico as "the most miserable I have ever known. I did not hear from my mother for several weeks. I did not like my father. And I did not know what to do about either of them."

When Hughes returned to Cleveland for his senior year of high school, he found turmoil both at home and in American society at large. World War I had ended, and white soldiers were coming home and looking for jobs. Black men like Homer, who had worked hard during the war years, were fired so the white men could have their jobs back. Racism was becoming more blatant, even in the North. Theaters and restaurants started banning African-American customers. In the meantime, he started to hear about the exciting things happening in Harlem, as a by-product of a movement called the Great Migration.

The Great Migration is the term used for the mass movement of millions of southern black people into the North and West of the United States between 1915 and 1960. The initial wave happened during World War I, when most of these migrants moved to major northern cities to find jobs in manufacturing and other war-related industries. Cities like Chicago, Detroit,

Harlem Renaissance painter Archibald Motley's painting, called *Black Belt*, depicts Harlem nightlife in the 1920s.

and Pittsburgh swelled in population. New York City became the unofficial destination for creative types, like jazz musicians, writers, poets, and sculptors. Having all of these black artists in one place created a "cultural explosion" known as the Harlem Renaissance. Hughes decided that Harlem was where he wanted to be, so he set his sights on attending Columbia University, which was nearby. The problem was that he didn't have enough money to attend, and his mother and stepfather certainly couldn't help him. When his father asked him to return to Mexico the summer after his high school graduation, although he had hated his time there the summer before, he decided he would go and ask his father for tuition money.

It was this second trip to Mexico that sealed Hughes's fate, although not in the way he was imagining at the time. As the train moved south, it passed over the Mississippi River, which is the second-longest in the United States at 2,340 miles (3,766 kilometers). It is also wide; crossing it would take some time. As the train moved slowly across the bridge, something clicked in Hughes's mind.

He started to think about the Mississippi's significance to African Americans in the United States. When slavery was a part of life, the phrase "being sold down the river" meant a slave was sold and sent farther down the Mississippi, farther into the Deep South and its harsher conditions. This led him to think about the rivers in Africa, from where those slaves had originally been taken, such as the Congo and the Nile, where people had lived along their banks because of the opportunities for trade and farming that they provided. He realized how black people's lives were entwined in different ways with the rivers in each country, and had been for generations, and he picked up the first piece of paper he could find, an envelope, and scribbled out the first few lines of a poem he later titled "The Negro Speaks of Rivers":

> I've known rivers:
> I've known rivers ancient as the world and older than the
>   flow of human blood in human veins.
>
> My soul has grown deep like the rivers.
> I bathed in the Euphrates when dawns were young.
> I built my hut near the Congo and it lulled me to sleep.
> I looked upon the Nile and raised the pyramids above it.
> I heard the singing of the Mississippi when Abe Lincoln
>   went down to New Orleans, and I've seen its muddy
>   bosom turn all golden in the sunset

He finished the poem in about fifteen minutes. It would become important for many reasons, not too far in the future.

TAKING STEPS TOWARD THE FUTURE

When Hughes arrived at his father's home in Mexico, he found a few changes. James Hughes had married his housekeeper, and he seemed slightly happier and more relaxed. He also didn't seem inclined to discuss his son's college plans, and he was gone on business quite a lot. As the end of the summer approached, Hughes finally broached the subject. James said he would be happy to pay for college—if Hughes went to Europe, learned several foreign languages, and took courses in engineering. He said Hughes could come back to Mexico afterward and find a job. When his son brought up the possibility of going to Columbia University instead, James not only refused to pay for tuition there, but he refused to pay for his son's ticket back home. Hughes was stuck in Mexico for nearly a year, until he could afford to leave on his own.

During this time, Hughes took odd jobs and taught English to make money. He also, possibly encouraged by his creation of "The Negro Speaks of Rivers," kept writing. He wrote poems, stories, and plays, and he began submitting them to a publication called the *Brownies' Book.* This was another magazine started by W. E. B. Du Bois, geared toward African-American children, to provide them with positive and appropriate entertainment. Its editor, a young woman named Jessie Fauset, liked Hughes's work and published it, and encouraged him to send her more. Eventually, that summer alone, Fauset published several of Hughes's poems, one short play, an essay, and a handful of short stories. When he sent her "The Negro Speaks of Rivers," she ensured that it was published, but not in the *Brownies' Book.* With Du Bois's permission, she put it into an issue of the *Crisis,* the magazine that Hughes's grandmother had introduced him to many years earlier.

For Hughes, this was a tremendous accomplishment, and it solidified his dreams of becoming a writer. Even James Hughes could not fail to be impressed by his son's accomplishment at having his work published in such a respectable and esteemed publication. He finally agreed that he would pay for Hughes's tuition at Columbia while Hughes pursued a writing career—although some historians think Hughes may have told his father that he would study engineering at Columbia instead.

The Brownies' Book

JUNE, 1921

$1.50 A YEAR   15cts. A COPY

An issue of the *Brownies' Book.*

Hughes finally left Mexico and headed back North, to what he was convinced was his destiny: Harlem, the New York City neighborhood that was a mecca for African-American creatives and the epicenter of the Harlem Renaissance. Writer James Weldon Johnson had proclaimed that New York was on the verge of becoming "the greatest Negro city in the world," and Hughes wanted to be a part of that greatness. But first, he had to get through Columbia University, and that proved to be more difficult than he had imagined.

CHAPTER TWO

A NEW START

When Langston Hughes arrived at Columbia University in 1921, he was full of hope and excitement. Finally, he was in New York City, close to the center of the action he sought. He had chosen the school "mainly because I wanted to see Harlem … More than Paris, or the Shakespeare country, or Berlin, or the Alps, I wanted to see Harlem, the greatest Negro city in the world." He described his arrival in the city as a revelation: as he exited the subway, he said, he "stood there, dropped [his] bags, took a deep breath and felt happy again."

A DREAM COME TRUE, A DISAPPOINTMENT

Unfortunately, Columbia University quickly put a stop to Hughes's feeling of hope. Even in one of the most cosmopolitan cities in the world, racism reared its ugly head. First, Hughes was told that

Opposite: This modern-day subway station is in the heart of Harlem.

One of Hughes's favorite places in Harlem was the public library.

they had never received a dorm room reservation for him. He felt it was because of his color; they hadn't realized that he was African American when he had made the arrangements. Instead, they had assumed he was from Mexico because he had sent his application from his father's home. Hughes stood his ground, and the administration relented and gave him a dorm room—making him the only African-American student in the dorms. Once again, he was very much a minority in a mostly white environment, just as he had been in Topeka. Things didn't improve much with time, either. As opposed to high school, where he had been popular, he found Columbia to be a somewhat hostile environment. Very few students were friendly, and when he tried to join the staff of the school newspaper, he was assigned to write social news— by an editor who knew that a black reporter would be banned from entering the dances and fraternity events he would be sent to cover. For the first time in his life, Hughes did not get good grades. Instead of focusing on schoolwork, he set out to explore New York City and experience its culture.

The famous period called the Harlem Renaissance was in its early years. The once-quiet neighborhood had nearly doubled in population between 1910 and the early 1920s as it became a cultural center for the black writers, artists, musicians, photographers, poets, and scholars who had come from the South seeking a new place where they could escape the oppression of segregation and express their talents. Hughes finally felt like he belonged, like he was part of a larger family—a family of intelligent, creative African Americans just like him.

His happiness at this feeling inspired him to write the poem "My People":

> The night is beautiful,
> So the faces of my people.
>
> The stars are beautiful,
> So the eyes of my people.
>
> Beautiful, also, is the sun.
> Beautiful, also, are the souls of my people.

It's no wonder, then, that Hughes spent more time in the city than on campus. He made the most of his time in New York. Due to his mother's influence and the circumstances of his early life, he had always loved books and the theater. One of his first stops in Harlem was the public library, where he was amazed and happy to find books written about black people, by black people. He attended Broadway shows and went to jazz clubs to hear music. He went to lectures at the Harlem branch of the library and met fellow poet Countee Cullen. And when the staff of the *Crisis*, which had continued to publish his work, realized he was now living in New York City, they insisted on meeting him. Once Hughes had met Fauset, Du Bois, and others who were active in the NAACP, he was invited to parties where he was introduced to other artists, intellectuals, and influential African Americans. He became part of the inner circle of people that would influence black thought in twentieth-century America. At least this part of his dreams of life in Harlem had come true. Still, at the end of his freshman year, Hughes decided to leave Columbia. He knew

The former library at Columbia University

he needed an education, but the Ivy League school made him miserable. His new plan was to see some of the world and meet more of his people.

The first thing Hughes had to do after dropping out of school was write his father to share the news. James, of course, was not happy with his son's decision. Some reports say that the two never communicated again, while some say that James offered to pay for another year of college and Hughes turned him down. Either way, Hughes was now on his own. His mother had never been a source of financial support; in fact, it was usually she who would ask him for money.

He got an apartment in Harlem, then had a difficult time finding work so he could pay his rent. Part of this was his age and his lack of a college degree, but the biggest barrier to finding a job that paid well was his race. He would look through the Help Wanted ads in the newspaper and see "No Colored Need Apply." Hughes ended up taking a job on a farm on Staten Island for several months, where he labored from dawn until dark. "We worked hard, ploughing, hoeing, spreading manure, picking weeds, washing lettuce, beets, carrots, onions, tying them and packing them for market," he remembered. Yet, he enjoyed this episode in his life; he liked the Greek family he worked for, and he got along with the other people that he worked with. Once the market season was over, though, so was his job.

Hughes decided to pursue another dream: to see other countries. He started working on freight ships down in the harbor in the hopes of traveling to faraway countries, but on his first gig, the ship never left New York. On his second one, though, he got lucky. He signed on as a member of the crew of the SS *West Hesseltine*, and soon he was on his way to Africa. He had wanted to see this continent since childhood, when his grandmother told him that it was where black people had come from. He felt he needed to go there to understand his race and his roots.

Hughes wasn't a sailor on the *West Hesseltine*. He was a messboy, assigned to the mess hall, or dining room, and his job was to clean it up. He also worked in the kitchen. Once again, this intelligent young man was working with his hands in a common position—but he liked it. He did very little writing during the voyage, but he was busy soaking up experiences that would influence his future writing for years to come.

Best of all, when they got to Africa, there was very little work to do. The shipping company hired locals to take care of business, believing that the American sailors would be unable to handle the heat on the African coast. Hughes, who had spent a hot, humid summer living in Chicago with his mother, didn't think it was so bad. He took advantage of his free time to explore and meet people.

Hughes found much beauty on the African continent, with its white-sand beaches and bright-green palm trees. He took in the colors and the eclectic styles of the clothing the people wore in the fifteen nations he visited. He thrilled to the sound of the music he heard and the dancing he saw. Yet, he was dismayed by the economic exploitation that he saw in action. Most of these nations were under the control of European countries like Belgium, England, and France. The natives worked to supply these countries with raw goods like fine mahogany and common spices, but they received little in return. They weren't even allowed to use the raw goods for themselves. Hughes couldn't help but compare this to the practice of slavery in the southern United States, which, after all, had only been illegal for just over fifty years at that point.

Hughes was in for another shock in Africa. He spent his time there visiting as many of the coastal nations as he could; he made it to fifteen in all, and he met and spoke to native people as he traveled. For the most part, he found them to be friendly, and they asked as many questions about life in America as he asked about life there. To his surprise, though, he discovered that they did not consider him to be a black man, because he was mixed race. One little boy, who had a white father and a black mother, told him that mulattoes were ignored in his culture and wanted to know if other people spoke to them in the United States. The native people also didn't understand, or were surprised to hear, that he considered himself to be even part African. To them, he was a white man. This was the opposite of the attitude in Jim Crow America, where anyone with even the smallest percentage of African ancestry was considered a person of color. Still, Hughes felt a kinship with the people he met, and he wrote his poem "Color" with them, and their pride in their dark skin, in mind:

Wear it
Like a banner
For the proud
Not like a shroud.
Wear it
Like a song
Soaring high
Not moan or cry.

Hughes was sorry to leave Africa, but he was ready for his next adventure. He arrived back in New York harbor, took a short trip to McKeesport, Pennsylvania, to visit his mother and the rest of the family—who were still in the habit of moving frequently—then returned to sign on for another journey, this time to the Netherlands.

Hughes liked that country so much that he signed on for a return journey after his first one was complete. This time, the crossing was rough and difficult. He decided it was time to take a break from life on the ocean and explore Europe for a while. He headed from the Netherlands to Paris, France, where he arrived almost broke but happy and excited to be in the city.

He worked a few odd jobs so he could pay rent on a cheap apartment, and he eventually found steady employment washing dishes in the kitchen of a nightclub called the Grand Duc. The best thing about this job, for Hughes, was the after-hours entertainment. Black musicians would show up after their regular gigs at other clubs, hang out, and play jazz, a developing new sound that was also finding popularity across the ocean in Harlem. Hughes started to develop an ear for its rhythms, which started to influence his poetry, as the blues once had. One of the best examples of this is his book-length poem, *Montage of a Dream Deferred*. While the full poem comprises ninety-one individually titled pieces, it is meant to be read as a single, long poem—in its original publishing run, it became a seventy-five-page book. Hughes described the poems' irregular rhythms and **onomatopoetic** bursts of sound in his preface to its original publication:

> In terms of current Afro-American popular music and the sources from which it progressed—jazz, ragtime, swing, blues, boogie-woogie, and be-bop—this poem on contemporary Harlem, like be-bop, is marked by conflicting changes, sudden nuances, sharp and impudent interjections, broken rhythms, and passages sometimes in the manner of a jam session,

THE CRISIS

A RECORD OF THE DARKER RACES

Volume One   NOVEMBER, 1910   Number One

Edited by W. E. BURGHARDT DU BOIS, with the co-operation of Oswald Garrison Villard, J. Max Barber, Charles Edward Russell, Kelly Miller, W. S. Braithwaite and M. D. Maclean.

CONTENTS

Along the Color Line   3

Opinion   7

Editorial   10

The N. A. A. C. P.   12

Athens and Browns-
ville 13
By MOORFIELD STOREY

The Burden . . . 14

What to Read . . 15

PUBLISHED MONTHLY BY THE

National Association for the Advancement of Colored People

AT TWENTY VESEY STREET   NEW YORK CITY

ONE DOLLAR A YEAR   TEN CENTS A COPY

An issue of the *Crisis*, to which Hughes was a regular contributor sometimes the popular song, punctuated by the riffs, runs, breaks, and distortions of the music of a community in transition.

In addition to enjoying the sights, sounds, and nightlife of Paris, Hughes continued to write and to send contributions to the *Crisis*, back in New York. He also, for a short time, pursued a relationship with a young woman named Anne-Marie Coussey (in some versions of the story, she is simply called Mary). She was British educated, of Scottish and African heritage, and allegedly the two discussed getting married. There are three official stories that explain the reason the romance ended. One is that while Coussey was impressed with Hughes's talent, she thought he needed to do more with his life, such as return to college. He resented the pressure he felt this put on him. Another version says that her father put an end to the relationship and sent her back to England because she came from money, and Hughes had nothing. The third variation is that Hughes told Coussey that he wasn't interested in marriage because it would interfere with his life as a poet. Whatever the reason, not only did Hughes and Coussey not marry, but Hughes never married anyone. He did, however, possibly immortalize his feelings for her in a few lines of his poem called "Fascination," which he wrote around the time of their relationship: "And because her skin is the brown of an oak leaf in autumn, but a softer color / I want to kiss her."

One other significant relationship that Hughes formed in France was with a Howard University professor named Alain Locke. Philadelphia-born Locke was a highly educated African American who had earned his PhD from Harvard and was always looking for talented black writers to promote. He and Hughes discussed the possibility of his using some of Hughes's work in an upcoming publication that he was editing. The two got along so well that they traveled to Italy together, but Hughes was running out of money. He decided it was time to return to the United States.

On the way back, however, he ran into a spot of trouble. On a train from Venice to Genoa, Hughes fell asleep, and although he had his passport and the last of his money pinned inside his shirt, he woke up to find them gone. He ended up staying in a low-rent boardinghouse until he could find a job on a ship bound for America, a mission that was complicated by the color of his skin. Many of the boats shipping out to the United States would not hire a black person. He did eventually find a ship that would take him on, but he also wrote one of his best-known and powerful poems in his depression over this blatant act of racism. "I, Too, Sing America" starts off with the lines, "I am the darker brother / They send me to eat in the kitchen / When company comes."

RENAISSANCE IN FULL SWING

Langston Hughes finally returned to New York City and his beloved Harlem in the fall of 1924. Within a few days, he attended a party in his honor—he hadn't realized that he was making quite a name for himself in the United States while living in Europe, thanks to the regular publication of his work in the *Crisis*. Apparently, a recent issue had featured an entire page of his poems because he had developed a steady readership. At the party, he met Charles S. Johnson, the editor of a new African-American magazine called the *Opportunity*. Jessie Fauset and W. E. B. Du Bois were there, too, of course. He also reacquainted himself with Countee Cullen, met fellow poets Arna Bontemps and James Weldon Johnson, and hit it off with Bontemps in particular. He discovered that Charles Johnson had begun throwing parties such as these to introduce African-American writers to the literary establishment, which was mostly white. Johnson correctly suspected that the white publishing world had no idea how many educated black writers were producing stories, poems, essays, and more, and he wanted to encourage a widening of horizons for everyone involved.

Hughes was not able to stay in New York at the time, however. His mother and brother were now living in Washington, DC, and Hughes felt obligated to join them—probably due to guilt or pressure from his mother. He also didn't have a job in New York and still could not support himself on money made from his writing. He hoped that while in DC he could arrange for a scholarship or a loan so he could return to school at Howard, the historical, all-black university located there.

Instead, he yet again took a series of menial jobs, trying to make enough money to help his family. It was while working as a busboy at the Wardman Park Hotel that he met two of the three people who would be most influential in launching his career. The first was a white poet named Vachel Lindsay. Lindsay was already famous both for his work and for giving dramatic readings of his poems. Because he believed that poetry was meant to be heard, not read, he often traveled the country, performing his pieces. He also included stage directions in some of them, in case someone else wanted to perform them.

When Hughes discovered that Lindsay was staying at the Wardman Park, he made a bold move. He collected some of his poems, wrote a note to accompany them, and laid them next to

Hughes in his busboy uniform

Lindsay's plate at his dining room breakfast table. Then he retreated to the kitchen and watched as the other poet sat down at his seat and picked up the papers. He couldn't see Lindsay's reaction, so he was shocked the next morning to discover that not only had Lindsay liked the poems, but he had performed them the night before during his own reading. Lindsay had even told newspaper reporters about this "busboy poet"—Hughes was greeted by photographers upon his arrival at work the next morning, and his picture appeared in the local paper the next day. The story was picked up by newspapers across the country, trumpeting Lindsay's new discovery. However, publicity didn't pay the bills. Hughes kept working at the Wardman Park—and he kept writing, too.

The second person to boost Hughes's career was a white novelist named Carl Van Vechten. Hughes had entered and won a poetry contest sponsored by Charles Johnson's magazine, the *Opportunity,* by submitting his poem titled "The Weary Blues." He attended the award ceremony in New York in May of 1925 to pick up his $40 prize and socialize with his friends and fellow award recipients including Countee Cullen and Zora Neale Hurston. At the after-party, Van Vechten approached him to ask if he had completed enough other poems to fill a whole book; when Hughes assured him he had, Van Vechten asked him to bring the poems over to his house the next day. After a few days of discussions and editing, Van Vechten sent the collection to his own illustrious publishing house, Alfred A Knopf. A few weeks later, he had secured a contract for Hughes, and Hughes's first book of poetry, titled *The Weary Blues,* was published in 1926. Hughes's career had officially been launched.

Carl Van Vechten was instrumental in launching Hughes's career.

The benefits of being the author of a critically acclaimed book were immediate. In addition to garnering positive reviews for his work, Hughes published—and was paid for—more poems in prestigious magazines like *Vanity Fair* and *New Republic*. He began to receive invitations from all over the country to read his works. Most importantly, he won a second poetry contest sponsored by a woman named Amy Spingarn. She was the wife of Joel Spingarn, one of the cofounders of the NAACP, for whom the organization's Spingarn Medal was named. Amy Spingarn was an artist herself, and she used her position as a wealthy man's wife to give financial support to up-and-coming black artists. After Hughes won the award she sponsored, she invited him to her home for tea. The two hit it off, and she believed in his work so strongly that she offered him an interest-free loan to go back to college. Hughes commented, "It was the happiest holiday gift I've ever received. My poems—through the kindness of this woman who liked poetry—sent me to college."

This time, Hughes chose to go to an all-male, all-African-American institution, Lincoln University, which was located near Oxford, Pennsylvania. Lincoln was one of the oldest colleges for African-American students in the United States, and it turned out professionals like doctors, lawyers, and scientists—it was nicknamed "the black Princeton." The rural campus was hundreds of miles away from his beloved Harlem, but Hughes enjoyed his years there. He joined a fraternity and had an active social life, but he also buckled down and took advantage of its academic opportunities. He took the train into Harlem on the weekends when he could, to take advantage of the nightlife and the company of his fellow creatives.

FAMOUS FRIENDS

Langston Hughes was not the only world-famous graduate of Lincoln University. His classmates included Cab Calloway, a celebrated jazz entertainer. Calloway was one of the world's most famous bandleaders for many years. He and his musicians took over as house band at the world-famous Cotton Club in Harlem after Duke Ellington and his orchestra vacated the position. Calloway also performed on stage and in films. He is possibly best known for his hit song "Minnie the Moocher."

Thurgood Marshall was also one of Hughes's classmates at Lincoln University. Marshall is perhaps most famous for winning the landmark *Brown v. Board of Education of Topeka, Kansas* case in 1954, which outlawed segregation in public schools. He went on to become the first African-American Supreme Court justice. He and Hughes actually interacted several times, including an incident where Hughes started a campus-wide discussion regarding whether the school should hire black teachers. It was put to a vote in one of his and Marshall's mutual classes, and Marshall voted against this suggestion. When Hughes found out, he was angry and confronted Marshall. He pointed out that Marshall had once expressed his anger over being discriminated against, so why would he discriminate against black professors? Marshall saw the wisdom in this, and the two discussed racial issues many times afterward.

Jazz musician Cab Calloway was one of Hughes's class-mates at Lincoln University.

Charlotte Osgood Mason

Hughes also continued to write, of course, and in his second year at Lincoln, he published his second book of poetry, called *Fine Clothes to the Jew*. (See Chapter Five for a discussion of the reactions generated by this book, its title, and its language.) That same year, he met the third person who would play an important role in his career, the woman who made it possible for him to write for a living. He was introduced to Charlotte Osgood Mason by Alain Locke. Mrs. Mason was a seventy-one-year-old white widow who, like Amy Spingarn, wanted to use her money to support African-American culture and its creators. After they had spent some time together, she became Hughes's patron. She gave him a $150 **stipend** each month (about $1,800 in today's dollars) so that he wouldn't have to work, which was supposed to encourage him to write productively. She even said she would pay for any travel related to his writing. All she asked in return was the chance to discuss his work with him. Sometimes this was a blessing, as when Mason encouraged Hughes to work on his first novel, *Not Without Laughter*, or when she recommended that he collaborate with another of her protégés, writer Zora Neale Hurston, on their play *Mule Bone*. But sometimes it was a curse, such as when he felt she was criticizing his work too much and attempting to influence his output, or when she demanded detailed accounts of how he spent the money she gave him. Ultimately, the situation became too problematic for Hughes. He didn't work well when forced to, and he wasn't feeling the emotions that usually spurred him in his work. The two eventually parted ways, but by then he was well on his way to making it on his own as a writer.

CHAPTER THREE

A LITERARY LIFE

Langston Hughes graduated with honors from Lincoln University in 1929, at the age of twenty-seven. Four months later, the stock market crashed, the Great Depression began, and the Roaring Twenties and the Harlem Renaissance both officially came to an end. Hughes was at a crossroads, and true to his nature, he took the road that led out of town.

ON THE MOVE AGAIN

In 1930, his semiautobiographical novel *Not Without Laughter* was published, and it won the Harmon Gold Award for Literature, which was given for distinguished achievement in the field. Along with an actual gold medal, winning the prize meant winning $400. As much as Hughes loved New York City and Harlem, he loved to travel, too. He took the money and headed to Cuba, then

Opposite: Hughes (*left*) poses with Charles S. Johnson (*right*) and three other friends on a Harlem rooftop during a party held in Hughes's honor.

Haiti, then to Cuba again, enveloping himself in Caribbean and Latin American music and culture, and being wined and dined by the intellectual elite. He also met and befriended up-and-coming Cuban and Haitian poets like Nicolás Guillén and Jacques Roumain. Guillén and Hughes had a similar way of incorporating native speech rhythms into their work and covered similar topics like racism. Roumain, like both of them, used his poetry to examine and express the folk motifs of his homeland. This was neither the first nor the last time Hughes would seek out and support fellow writers. Perhaps he felt he could pay back all of the help and encouragement he received over the years.

Hughes re-entered the United States in 1931 and took the time to stop and meet with Mary McLeod Bethune, the president of Bethune-Cookman College in Florida. Bethune was a mover and shaker in the field of educational opportunities for African Americans. She established the college—then called Daytona Normal and Industrial Institute—in 1904 to provide a school for African-American girls. A force for civil rights, she served as the president of the Florida chapter of the National Association of Colored Women for many years and later started the National Council of Negro Women. She worked for several presidents in various advisory and committee positions, and when she became the director of the Division of Negro Affairs of the National Youth Administration, she also became the first African-American woman in history to head a federal agency. It's no wonder that when she spoke to him about his career and his future, Hughes listened. He had great respect for her accomplishments.

Unlike Charlotte Mason, however, Bethune didn't attempt to bully or manipulate Hughes. The two of them sat and chatted on Bethune's front porch, where her warmth and charm put him at ease, as she spoke to him about where he could go next in his career—literally. She proposed that he should tour the country, sharing his poetry with all audiences. She pointed out that he could be an inspiration to other poor people of color, proving that dreams can come true no matter what a person's beginnings in life and also that not all poets were white. She reminded him that he could provide many people with a source of entertainment and education that they could not afford otherwise.

Hughes left Florida inspired. He had always sought out the "real people" of the countries where he traveled, attempting to get to know them and how they thought. This was a chance to combine that habit with his love for travel.

His first step down this new road in his career was to apply for a **grant** from the Rosenwald Foundation, established by Sears, Roebuck and Company president Julius Rosenwald for the "well being of mankind" in 1917. In addition to supporting organizations such as the University of Chicago and the Museum of Science and Industry in Chicago, and giving millions of dollars to other schools, colleges and universities, museums, hospitals, and clinics, Rosenwald earmarked large sums of money to improve the situation of African Americans in the United States. The foundation built schools in poor, rural, primarily black school districts all over the South.

When Hughes requested money from the foundation, he explained his intent to travel throughout the country, especially the South, speaking to audiences that had never seen an African-American author before—if they even knew such a thing existed. He explained his plan to sell inexpensive versions of his poetry books, and he even prepared a display about black authors from around the world to bring with him. He quoted Bethune and

Mary McLeod Bethune

said he wanted to "bring poetry to the people." The Rosenwald Foundation gave him $1,000 to launch his tour, which he used to buy a car, print low-cost editions of his books, and update his display.

Hughes spent months driving through the South and out West, performing his readings at churches, colleges, community centers, and schools in an attempt to reach as many ages and classes of people as possible. After beginning in Pennsylvania, he toured the Deep South, making stops in Alabama, Georgia, South Carolina, and Tennessee, even though he knew it could be dangerous for a man of color to be seen as too successful or confident in those states. He spread out to Kansas, Missouri, Oklahoma, and Texas. He stopped in Arizona and New Mexico and officially ended the tour in California. He often took less than his initial fee of $100 in smaller, poorer communities, and sometimes he read for free. He was energized by the experience, reporting back to the foundation, "I've never had a finer response anywhere, or met more beautiful people. Even in the backwoods, they seemed to know what I was talking about, and to appreciate it."

Hughes made a point of stopping in Daytona, Florida, to do a special reading at Bethune-Cookman College so he could show Bethune how he had carried out her proposal. As the tour was coming to an end, he also embarked on a new project with his friend and fellow poet, Arna Bontemps: a children's book called *Popo and Fifina*. The book was the first of many collaborations between the two.

Then Hughes, the poet and author, received the opportunity to try a new skill: screenwriting. His friend and colleague Louise Thompson asked him if he wanted to travel to the Soviet Union to work on a movie, and he jumped at the chance. African Americans were not offered jobs writing movies in the United States. Plus, he was curious to see a new country and learn more about the Soviets' **socialist** form of government.

HUGHES MEETS MOTHER RUSSIA

When Hughes and Thompson arrived in Moscow, the capital of the Soviet Union, they and the other twenty people in their party were treated like celebrities. Then they learned that the script for the movie, to be titled *Black and White*, didn't yet have an outline. They signed contracts for four months of guaranteed work, then discovered that they didn't have to work for at least thirty days, until the outline arrived.

When it did, Hughes knew the project was in trouble. First, the outline was written in Russian and needed to be translated. The director, who was German, didn't speak Russian or English and had no experience. Finally, the storyline of the film, **ostensibly** about race relations between blacks and whites in the South, turned out to be a ridiculous socialist fantasy. While discussions about these problems were ongoing, Hughes and Thompson read a newspaper article stating that influential Americans in Moscow had found out about the movie and were outraged that the Soviets wanted to produce a film that was critical of the United States. They sent word back to the US government, who in turn threatened not to recognize the legitimacy of the Soviet government if the movie project went forward. The Communist leadership wanted to be recognized by the American government, so they cancelled the project. To appease the actors and crew they had assembled, they offered full-paid tours of the country or tickets home, in addition to the money they had already paid everyone to do almost nothing. Hughes, not surprisingly, chose to tour the country.

At this point in his life, Hughes was doing fairly well as an author. He wasn't rolling in money, but he was making a steady income from translations and multiple printings of his novel and his poetry books. He was getting good reviews for his two children's books—a collection of poetry called *The Dream Keeper and Popo and Fifina*—so he was getting **advances** from publishers to work on new projects. While on the tour of the eastern Soviet Union, he wrote articles for various Russian publications, so he was making money as he went. However, he never forgot that in the United States he was a black man and therefore seen as inferior. He had seen such attitudes in other countries, too, so he was pleasantly surprised to see an apparent absence of racism under the socialist regime in the Soviet Union.

He saw dark-skinned people who held important jobs and were treated as professionals. He saw members of other minority ethnic groups and religions being allowed to participate in civic life. He saw women experiencing new freedoms in a society that had once allowed brides to be purchased and forced women to wear veils. He discovered that public transportation was no longer segregated. Hughes thought all of this was wonderful. His praise and admiration for the Soviets and their new society would come back to haunt him later.

When Hughes landed stateside again in the summer of 1933, he had been out of the country for over a year. He discovered that the country was still in economic crisis, so profits from his books were almost nonexistent. He had no place to live and no definite plans for his immediate future. He was saved once again by the generosity of a wealthy patron, this time a San Francisco

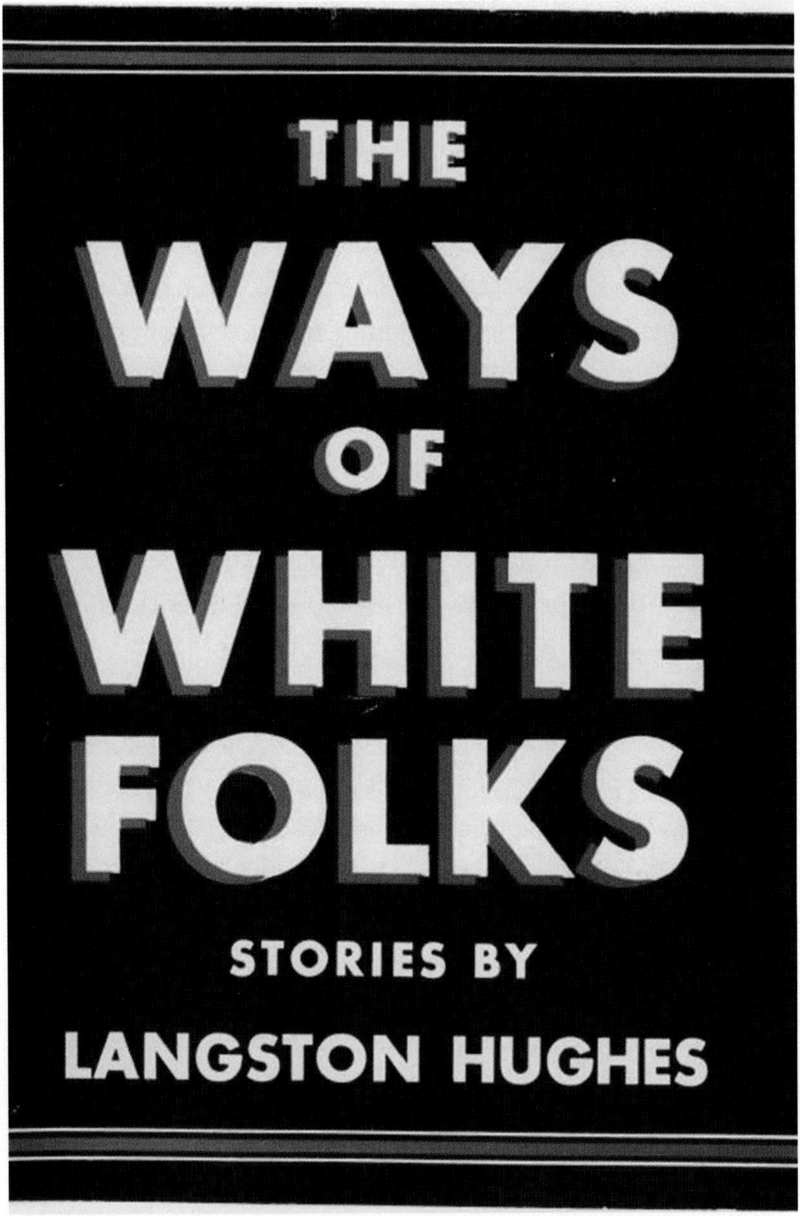

THE
WAYS
OF
WHITE
FOLKS

STORIES BY

LANGSTON HUGHES

Hughes wrote this collection of short stories during his stay in Carmel, California.

man named Noel Sullivan, who offered Hughes the use of his vacation home in Carmel, California, for a year. Sullivan even provided Hughes with food and a cook.

Hughes settled into this quiet, beachside community—founded as an artists' colony, now mostly a retirement community for wealthy people—and buckled down to business. He wanted to write a travel book based on his experiences in Asia—which he had toured after the movie project fell apart in the Soviet Union—and attempted to put together a book of poems written about his impressions of the Soviet Union. His publisher rejected both, though, criticizing them as **propaganda** and admonishing Hughes that such works were beneath his artistic talents.

He sold stories to magazines like *Harper's, the New Yorker,* and *Scribner's* to keep money coming in, partially so he could send some to his mother. In the meantime, he ended up with better results on his next book, a collection of short stories called *The Ways of White Folks,* for which he once again received critical acclaim—and enough money to enable him to devote himself to writing still more.

While in California, Hughes attracted some negative attention for joining the local chapter of the John Reed Club, a national organization sponsored by the US Communist Party and formed to support **leftist** and **Marxist** artists and writers. His interest in the club probably stemmed from his experiences in the Soviet Union, which were obviously still on his mind. He was an active member, too, participating in fundraisers and rallies and writing about labor and socialist issues.

Hughes was a prolific writer in many genres.

Hughes's **idyllic** stay in California ended when he received word that his father had died, at the age of sixty-three. His presence was requested in Mexico for the reading of the will, and he went, although he suspected, correctly as it turns out, that his father hadn't left him anything. However, his father's business partners had inherited some money from James, and they insisted on sharing a portion with Hughes. True to form, he spent the money almost right away, using it to live in Mexico for several months. This time, he enjoyed himself. He went out to parties and nightclubs and hobnobbed with other writers and artists. He listened to music and wrote new poetry and worked on translating his older poems into Spanish. When he ran out of money, he returned to the United States, this time to his favorite stomping grounds: New York City.

Hughes hadn't been back to New York in nearly three years, and he was surprised and flattered to discover that one of his plays, *Mulatto*, was about to open on Broadway. His agent had forgotten to tell him—or send him the contracts. Hughes had to sign them as soon as possible. After he did, he realized that the play had been radically changed in its adaptation from the page to the stage. He tried not to let it bother him, but the play received terrible reviews. Still, it ran for over a year, setting a record for the longest Broadway run of any play by an African-American author, a record that stood until 1958.

Perhaps to give himself more control over future productions of his plays, Hughes worked with Louise Thompson to establish the Harlem Suitcase Theater in 1938. He later founded the New Negro Theater in Los Angeles and the Skyloft Players in Chicago. His aim was to give African Americans a place to learn playwriting and performing skills.

By 1937, Hughes had published poems, novels, plays, articles, and short stories, but he was feeling the effects of a slump and was not selling enough new material to live on. As he usually did when he was feeling blocked, he took a trip. He returned to Paris for the first time since 1924. While the nightclubs were still active, he felt a sense of seriousness and almost desperation that was new. Like the United States, many countries in Europe were experiencing economic depression. Spain was in a civil war.

It was at a meeting of the International Writers' Congress in Paris that Hughes got involved in the issues that were plaguing Spain. He ended up traveling to Spain with his old friend Nicolás Guillén, who had become a journalist, and he himself became a war correspondent. The *Afro-American*, a newspaper based in Baltimore, Maryland, paid him to cover the war from the front, especially stories about the black Americans serving in the Lincoln Brigade. The International Brigades, which included the Lincoln, were groups of foreign volunteers who were recruited to fight on the Republican side, called the Loyalists, against the Nationalists. The Nationalists, led by Generalissimo Francisco Franco, were trying to overthrow the legally elected government. Franco had the army, the church, and the wealthy on his side. However, the Loyalists were made up mostly of the "common people," bolstered by support from the International Brigades. In addition to the United States and Canada, many European countries sent volunteers to participate in the brigades, including Austria, Belgium, Czechoslovakia, France, Hungary, Poland, the United Kingdom, and Yugoslavia. Looking back, this three-year war was a precursor to World War II.

Reporting from Madrid amid the sights and sounds of bombing and gunfire, Hughes also wrote for the *Alianza de Intelectuales Antifascistas,* or Alliance of Antifascist Intellectuals, through which he met other American writers who were helping the Loyalist cause, like Ernest Hemingway. He stayed for six months, longer than he had intended, fascinated by the parallels between Spaniards fighting for freedom in their home country and African Americans in the United States fighting for the same thing. He left Spain feeling energized and compelled to write poetry again. Hughes started with a series of six poems inspired by what he saw, including "We Captured a Wounded Moor Today," "Air Raid: Barcelona," "Song of Spain," and "Madrid, 1937."

A CHANGE IN PERSPECTIVE

Hughes returned to his former prolific self after his sojourn in Spain. He wrote and directed a play called *Don't You Want to Be Free?* which was once described as "the most remarkable theatrical work of his career." Produced at the Suitcase Theater, the show wove together short, dramatic scenes with poetry, blues songs, spirituals, and sermons. Hughes wanted it to be both educational and entertaining, and the show was a huge hit.

He then took another stab at screenwriting, this time in the United States on a legitimate project. His friend Arna Bontemps's novel *God Sends Sunday* was being made into a movie, and Hughes was asked to help adapt it. He didn't care for the experience, however, saying that "Hollywood has spread in exaggerated form every ugly and ridiculous stereotype of the deep South's conception of Negro characters." He never worked on another movie again.

Hughes published the first of his two autobiographies in 1940. *The Big Sea* covered his life up until the age of twenty-nine. Though the book got good reviews, its sales numbers were low. Hughes was already on to bigger and better things, though: he signed on with the Writers' War Board to do his part for the war effort when the United States entered World War II in 1941. He wrote articles for army newspapers and composed lyrics for songs to be performed at rallies.

INFLUENCES

The three poets that Langston Hughes consistently named as his greatest influences were Carl Sandburg, Walt Whitman, and Paul Laurence Dunbar.

Carl Sandburg (1878–1967) One of Hughes's high-school English teachers introduced him to Sandburg's work. Sandburg was famous for writing free verse poetry, which inspired Hughes to give his own poetry a try. The two men both grew up in the Midwest, and they both wrote about their versions of America. Hughes later referred to Sandburg as his "guiding star" and said the other poet was his "greatest influence in the matter of form." Hughes even wrote a poem about Sandburg that appeared in his first autobiography, *The Big Sea*.

Walt Whitman (1819–1892) Considered one of America's most influential poets, Whitman wrote one great book of poetry, *Leaves of Grass*, which he rewrote and revised several times throughout his life. His mission was to create a new and distinctly American form of poetry. Hughes paid homage to Whitman with his poem "I, Too, Sing America," which was in a way a response to Whitman's poems "I Hear America Singing" and "Song of Myself."

Paul Laurence Dunbar (1872–1906) Another midwesterner, Dunbar was one of the first African-American poets to gain praise for his work in America. Like Hughes, Dunbar wrote literature in all of its forms: poems, novels, newspaper articles, short stories, song lyrics, and more. He was also known for his use of dialect to capture the African-American experience. Critics and historians alike say that

Walt Whitman

Dunbar's work in the late nineteenth century would prove influential to the development of the Harlem Renaissance in the 1920s and 1930s. He also influenced writers such as James Weldon Johnson and Countee Cullen, in addition to Langston Hughes.

Poetry continued to be the form in which he produced the most. In the 1940s, he published two collections, *Shakespeare in Harlem* and *Fields of Wonder*. *Montage of a Dream Deferred* was published in 1951.

The cover of Hughes's first autobiography

Hughes also took on an all-new type of project. He started writing a series of short stories about a character named Jesse B. Semple, also called Simple. The stories originally appeared in a column he wrote for the *Chicago Defender*, a weekly African-American newspaper, and later in the *New York Post*. Simple was an "African-American Everyman," dealing with the everyday ups and downs, frustrations and triumphs of being a black man in America. Hughes made the stories funny and warm while making points about racist obstacles. Simple became a hugely popular character, and Hughes wrote stories about him for twenty-three years. They were eventually compiled into three books: *Simple Speaks His Mind, Simple Takes a Wife*, and *Simple Stakes a Claim*. He even wrote the book and lyrics for a musical based on the character, called *Simply Heavenly*, which was performed in New York City, Washington, DC, and various cities in Europe in the late 1950s. The show had a revival in 1987 in Philadelphia and another in London in 2003.

Hughes published his second autobiography, *I Wonder as I Wander*, in 1956, when he was only fifty-four years old. It has the flavor of a **travelogue** or a memoir, as he recounts his travel experiences through Cuba, Haiti, Russia, Soviet Central Asia, Japan, and Spain throughout the 1930s. It may have seemed premature for a man of his age, who was still active in his field, to have written one autobiography, let alone a second. However, when he was only in his forties, Hughes was already considered an elder statesman of American literature, probably because he had been publishing for so long.

During this time, he started to turn his attention to the outside world while continuing to produce his own work, and he took influential positions when they were offered, such as

There are words like *Freedom*
Sweet and wonderful to say.
On my heartstrings freedom sings
All day everyday.

There are words like *Liberty*
That almost make me cry.
If you had known what I know
You would know why.

- Langston Hughes (1902 -1967), "Words Like Freedom"

This plaque on East Forty-First Street in New York City immortalizes Hughes's poem "Words Like Freedom."

poet-in-residence at Atlanta University in 1947 and poet-teacher at the University of Chicago in 1949. Hughes was also asked to translate other poets' works into English, including those of his friends Guillén and Roumain. He worked with Arthur Spingarn, president of the NAACP, to write a history of the organization called *Fight for Freedom: The Story of the NAACP*. It was published in 1962, just five years before Hughes died.

Hughes started to receive important awards, such as the Spingarn Medal, given annually by the NAACP for outstanding achievement by an African American. The award, an actual gold medal, was created in 1914 by Joel Elias Spingarn—Amy Spingarn's husband, Arthur's brother, and the chairman of the board of the NAACP. Arthur Spingarn himself presided over the ceremony when Hughes received his medal.

In 1961, Hughes was inducted into the National Institute of Arts and Letters (now merged with the American Academy of Arts and Letters), which is considered the highest formal recognition of artistic merit in the United States. He was only the second African American to receive this honor; the first was his longtime acquaintance W. E. B. Du Bois.

Langston Hughes died on May 22, 1967, of complications from cancer and heart disease. He had been feeling ill for some time, but he resisted going to see a doctor. By the time he was diagnosed, it was too late. Mourners gathered for his funeral, which he had dictated should be a celebratory affair, complete with a jazz band. He injected his infamous sense of humor into the proceedings, having a friend read his supposed last words: "Tell all my mourners / To mourn in red— / 'Cause there ain't no sense / In my bein' dead," and picking the last song to be played at the service: "Do Nothing till You Hear from Me."

On the more serious side, Arna Bontemps gave an informal eulogy of sorts and read some of Hughes's poems, and his other friends read "The Negro Speaks of Rivers" as his body was cremated. Twenty-four years after he died, his ashes were interred in the Schomburg Center for Research in Black Culture, which is located in his beloved Harlem. A special tile marks the spot.

PART II

The Work of Langston Hughes

"My soul has grown deep like the rivers."

—*Langston Hughes*

Opposite: Langston Hughes wrote in many mediums throughout his career, including poetry, short stories, novels, plays, and memoirs.

CHAPTER FOUR

A LIFETIME OF WORK

Langston Hughes may have described his literary output best when he said: "My writing has been largely concerned with the depicting of Negro life in America." Whether writing poetry, novels, articles, plays, or musicals, Hughes explored the struggles and problems faced by African Americans in the United States. As author Alice Walker explained, in the children's book she wrote about Hughes:

> He always wrote truthfully about black people. He showed that they were beautiful, and sometimes ugly, like most people. He showed that they were sometimes happy and sometimes sad—and that they could laugh even when they were feeling blue. He always thought this ability made them special.

Opposite: Langston Hughes in his native Harlem, in 1958

In fact, even though he published sixteen books of poetry; three collections of short stories; two autobiographies; two novels; about twenty plays, musicals and operettas; eight children's books; three history books; and countless newspaper and magazine articles, Hughes lived by the dictate "write what you know." And what he knew best was what it was like to be a black man in the early- to mid-twentieth century.

The Academy of American Poets website points out that "Hughes refused to differentiate between his personal experience and the common experience of black America. He wanted to tell the stories of his people in ways that reflected their actual culture, including both their suffering and their love of music, laughter, and language itself."

Hughes used his personal life as inspiration for larger statements on universal experience. He did this because he wanted African Americans to be proud of themselves, and he wanted to try to show whites what it felt like to be a black person in the United States. On a larger scale, he wanted to shed light on the injustices of segregation and racism, to inspire people to think and to examine their feelings, and to bring about equality for all people.

Poetry

Hughes is most famous for his poems. They seemed to be the best and easiest way for him to express his thoughts and feelings. Critic and biographer Arnold Rampersad describes three distinct thematic areas into which Hughes's poetry can be divided: isolation, despair, and suicide; socialism; and the voice of black people and their needs. That third category can be subdivided again, into works that protest the social conditions of blacks; those that celebrate the beauty and dignity of the race; and those that affirm the dignity and social significance of African Americans. Most of Hughes's best-known poems fall into one or more of those categories.

For example, in "The Negro Speaks of Rivers," written when he was eighteen years old and first published in the *Crisis*, Hughes ponders the role of these bodies of water in the lives of black people when he writes, "I've known rivers ancient as the world and older than the flow of human blood in human veins."

In an early work called "When Sue Wears Red," his high school crush is described as looking like "a queen from some time-dead Egyptian night." He goes on to sigh that "the beauty of Susanna Jones in red / burns in my heart a love-fire sharp like pain."

In "The Weary Blues," the poem that brought his work to the attention of Carl Van Vechten, Hughes describes an old man playing the blues on the piano. He uses words like "dull," "pallor," "moan," and "melancholy" to create a mood before he even writes the words the old man is singing:

> I heard that Negro sing, that old piano moan—
> "Ain't got nobody in all this world,
> Ain't got nobody but ma self.
> I's gwine to quit ma frownin'
> And put ma troubles on the shelf."

These verses also highlight Hughes's use of colloquial language and his imitation of the rhythms and themes of blues music. This was one of the poems that Hughes slipped to Vachel Lindsay in the dining room of the Wardman Park Hotel.

In 1951, Hughes looked around at the people of Harlem, who seemed to represent African Americans all over the country in their frustrations, and asked difficult questions. After World War II, black men who had fought for America returned from the war to continued racism, segregation, unemployment, and poverty. Whose democracy had they fought for?

In *Montage of a Dream Deferred*, Hughes presents a panorama of Harlem life, standing in for African-American life, using the sounds and methods of contemporary African-American music. A montage is defined as "an artistic work that consists of smaller

The cover of an illustrated version of Hughes's famous poem

pieces of art combined into a unified whole that reveals a larger picture or meaning." This is an accurate description of *Montage of a Dream Deferred*, in which Hughes uses recurring themes and phrases throughout shorter poems that make up the book; in fact, the book begins and ends with the same two lines: "Good morning, daddy! / Ain't you heard?"

One of Hughes's most famous poems from the montage is "Harlem," which is sometimes called "A Dream Deferred" after its famous opening line: "What happens to a dream deferred? / Does it dry up / like a raisin in the sun?"

Playwright Lorraine Hansberry named her most famous work, *A Raisin in the Sun,* which was the first-ever Broadway play written by an African-American woman, after the line in this poem; her play explores some of the same themes as the poem, such as the importance of dreams to the survival of human beings.

"Harlem" also sums up the frustrations that many black people were feeling at that time in Jim Crow America. Despite the fact that slavery had been legally abolished and laws had been established that were supposed to guarantee equality for African Americans, the reality of life was that black people went to inferior, segregated schools, had to settle for menial jobs, and were banned from using the same public facilities as white people. The landmark Supreme Court case that would end segregation was still three years away, and its implementation would take even longer.

Another of Hughes's most well-known works covers similar ground. "I, Too, Sing America," which may have been written in response to Walt Whitman's "I Hear America Singing," is written from the perspective of an African-American man in the

Columbia Pictures
presents
SIDNEY
POITIER
in
a raisin in the sun
with
CLAUDIA McNeil · RUBY DEE

Screenplay by LORRAINE HANSBERRY from her play
Produced on the stage by PHILIP ROSE and DAVID J. COGAN
Produced by DAVID SUSSKIND and PHILIP ROSE
Directed by DANIEL PETRIE

Lorraine Hansberry's play, turned into a movie in 1961, got its name from
Hughes's poem "Harlem."

Jim Crow South. It illustrates the pain and hurt of segregation
while ending with a feeling of hope. Today, Hughes writes, the
"darker brother" gets sent to eat in the kitchen when company
comes, but he will "grow strong," and tomorrow he will be at the
table. With a last note of defiant pride, the narrator says, "They'll
see how beautiful I am / And be ashamed."

When critic Donald B. Gibson wrote "During the twenties when most American poets were turning inward, writing obscure and esoteric poetry to an ever decreasing audience of readers, Hughes was turning outward, using language and themes, attitudes and ideas familiar to anyone who had the ability simply to read," he may well have been talking about "My People" and "Color," two short works that use deceptively simple language and structure to get their point across.

In the three two-line stanzas of "My People," Hughes compares the darkness of the night to the faces of his people, describing both as "beautiful." However, he also compares his people to the sun, which mirrors the dignity and brilliance of their souls. "Color" uses twenty-three words in unstructured verse to express Hughes's opinion that African Americans should be proud of whatever color they are.

"The Negro Mother" is a longer piece, told in a mother's voice. It is atypical of Hughes's work, because it is written in rhyme, almost songlike. The narrator of the piece is a female slave who calls herself the mother of all Negroes and says she has persevered because, as a black woman, she is the hope of the race. She encourages black Americans to continue to struggle for freedom. Her calming tone and her allusion to nurturing without complaint contrasts with the brutal reality of the story she is telling about the history of slavery.

Plays

Hughes wrote approximately twenty plays, most of which were only moderately successful. One exception was a work he didn't even know was going to be performed on Broadway almost until it happened: *Mulatto*.

LANGSTON HUGHES'S PEERS

Langston Hughes was not the only poet or writer associated with the Harlem Renaissance, of course. Three of his peers were Arna Bontemps, Countee Cullen, and Claude McKay. Who were they?

Arna Bontemps (1902–1973) One of Hughes's best friends and most frequent collaborators, Bontemps was also mixed-race, also got his start by publishing poems in *Crisis* magazine (and later *Opportunity*), and also won prizes from both publications. His first novel, *God Sends Sunday*, was criticized for its emphasis on the more unpleasant side of black life, something Hughes faced also. Bontemps was better known for his novels and children's books (two of which he wrote with Hughes) than his poetry.

Countee Cullen (1903–1946) Like Langston Hughes, Cullen was raised partially by his grandmother and started writing poetry at a young age; he was already winning writing awards while in high school. He also wrote novels, plays, and children's books. Quite unlike Hughes, Cullen had a traditional educational path, attending New York University, where he graduated Phi Beta Kappa in 1925, followed by a master's degree from Harvard University. Although Cullen and Hughes often competed for prizes in contests, their styles were very different: Cullen used traditional European writing structures and verse. And because he was raised and educated in a primarily white community, his critics argued that he lacked the background to comment from personal experience on the lives of other African Americans or write about popular "black themes."

Claude McKay (1889–1948) Like Hughes, McKay used his work to establish himself as a literary voice for social justice, using his poetry to express his social and political concerns from his perspective as a black man in the United States. Born in Jamaica, McKay learned the more traditional forms of British poetry, such as sonnets, but he wrote some of his poems in his native Jamaican dialect.

Mulatto was written in the early 1930s and illustrated the issues of mixed-race people and parental rejection—very personal themes for Hughes. In its initial production, the play set a record for the number of performances of a play written by an African American, but the play's producer changed the written play by adding a rape scene and other sensational elements that Hughes hadn't written to make it sell better on Broadway. The play was so controversial that it was banned in Philadelphia. Hughes was unhappy with the changes but couldn't do anything about it.

He also ran into problems with the production of the play *Mule Bone*, which he wrote in collaboration with Zora Neale Hurston. Subtitled "A Comedy of Negro Life" and set in Eatonville, Florida—Hurston's hometown—this farcical play focuses on a love triangle between Jim and Dave, partners in a song-and-dance team, and a woman named Daisy. The title comes from the fact that Jim hits Dave with a mule bone during a fit of jealousy. Religion comes into play, as factions from the town's two churches each defend a different member of the dispute. The story was based on a folk tale and written in **vernacular**. Shortly after the play's creation, Hurston copyrighted the play in her name only. Hughes was furious. The two had a tremendous fight and never spoke to each other again. Hughes had to sue Hurston to have his writing credit added, and because a legal battle ensued, the play could not be produced during either writer's lifetime. The debut production was staged at the Lincoln Center Theater in New York City in 1991—sixty years after it was written.

Novels

Long-form writing was not Hughes's forte, so he only wrote two novels. His first, published in 1930, was written during the last

A scene from *Mule Bone*, the play Hughes wrote with Zora Neale Hurston

year or so of his college years at Lincoln University, while he was still under the patronage of Charlotte Mason. It was probably only the pressure she exerted that got Hughes to finish the book at all. *Not Without Laughter* won the Harmon Gold Medal for literature. The book is semi-autobiographical, based on many of the people, places and experiences that informed Hughes's childhood in Lawrence, Kansas. The protagonist of the book is a boy whose family deals with multiple struggles imposed upon them due to their race and class on top of the usual family issues with relating to one another. Hughes said:

> I wanted to write about a typical Negro family in the Middle West, about people like those I had known in Kansas. But mine was not a typical Negro family.

In other words, he had to invent or imagine a typical family for the sake of the story.

Tambourines to Glory, his second novel, is based on his musical of the same name. Some people complain that it's not really a novel at all, since he didn't add much to the stage script. It lacks elements like extended descriptive passages and characters' unspoken thoughts and reads more like a script than a narrative.

Short Stories

In his second autobiography *I Wonder as I Wander*, Hughes related the story of how reading the short stories of D. H. Lawrence inspired him to try his own hand at the genre. In 1934, he succeeded when he published *The Ways of White Folks*. This collection of fourteen stories is a running social commentary on the suffering the black community endures at the hands of white society. Sometimes humorous and sometimes tragic, the stories share an overall tone of pessimism.

Hughes published a few other short-story collections, but they are far less famous and successful than his three collections of stories about Jessie B. Semple, the character he created for the *Chicago Defender*. *Simple Speaks His Mind* has been described as "a collection of entertaining Harlem conversations ... You learn here at first hand what it really means to be a man of color in the land of the free and the home of the brave." The *Kirkus Review* summed up the book, saying, "Simple airs his views over women, taxes, unemployment, government, Jim Crowism, religion, sex, and The Law, with the moot problem of race relations a constant itch."

Carl Van Vechten himself reviewed *Simple Takes a Wife* for the *New York Times*, and he opened the review by saying:

> It is not as generally known as it should be that Langston Hughes laughs with, cries with, and speaks for, the Negro (in all classes) more understandingly, perhaps, than any other writer ... *Simple Takes a Wife* is a superior achievement to the first of the series ... The new book is more of a piece, the material is more carefully and competently arranged, more unexpectedly presented; it is more brilliant, more skillfully written, funnier, and perhaps just a shade more tragic than its predecessor.

In its review of the third book in the series, *Simple Stakes a Claim*, the *New York Times* included part of the foreword that Hughes wrote for the book:

> The race problem in America is serious business, I admit. But must it always be written about seriously? So many weighty volumes, cheerless novels, sad abstracts and violent books have been written on race relations, that I would like to see some writers of both races write about our problems with black tongue in white cheek, or vice versa. Sometimes I try. Simple helps me.

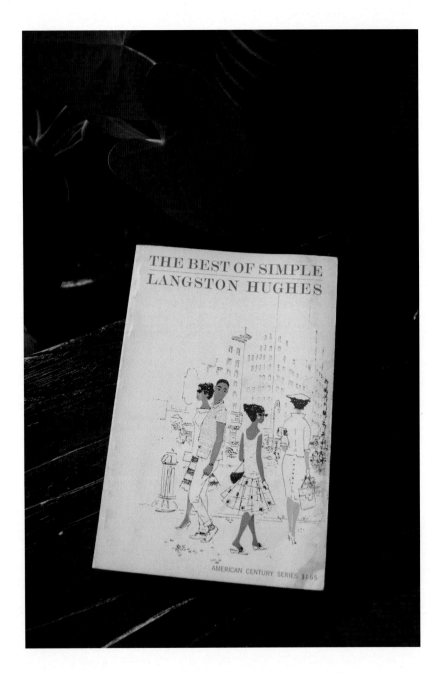

This compilation of Hughes's stories about Simple was published in 1961.

The reviewer goes on to say:

> Like its predecessors, *Simple Stakes a Claim* is funny and sharp and indignant and tolerant, even of whites; and full of veiled warnings and demonstrations of the stupidities, callousness and cruelties of both whites and Negroes (but more of whites than of Negroes; the other would hardly have been expected, nor would it have been accurate as things are) … In one form or another throughout, he lightly tans the hide of segregation.

Autobiographies

Some people may think a thirty-eight-year-old man is too young to write his autobiography. However, Hughes had no shortage of experiences to write about. *The Big Sea*, the first of his two autobiographies, covers his experiences in both Paris and New York during the Roaring Twenties. As the publisher's description of the book says, Hughes came of age in the early 1920s and had many memorable escapades and experiences in the "two great playgrounds of the decade"—Harlem and Paris. In *The Big Sea*, he recounts those memorable years, when he lived in Paris and worked as a cook and waiter in nightclubs, and when he lived in Harlem, known as a rising young poet at the center of the Harlem Renaissance.

Hughes's second autobiography, published when he was fifty-four, focuses on his adult life. *I Wonder as I Wander* begins with Hughes's blunt assessment of his young adult life:

When I was twenty-seven, the stock-market crash came. When I was twenty-eight, my personal crash came. Then I guess I woke up. So, when I was almost thirty, I began to make my living from writing.

The book, which he describes as an autobiographical journey, is full of stories about Hughes's trips through multiple countries from 1930 to 1937. Readers enjoy it because he writes about almost every experience with his typical good humor and passion.

Children's Books

Most people are surprised to hear that Langston Hughes wrote books for children. For his two most famous, he collaborated with his longtime friend Arna Bontemps.

The first one was titled *Popo and Fifina: Children of Haiti*. This picture book was almost universally praised. It was called an early African-American classic and a milestone in the history of literature for children. The story is simple, telling the tale of two young siblings, Popo and Fifina, who move from their home in the hills of Haiti to a town by the sea. The story revolves around their reaction to their new home, and follows them on a trip back to the hills for a visit, a trip to the lighthouse at the end of the island, and an amazing tropical storm.

The second of Hughes and Bontemps's books for children, *The Pasteboard Bandit*, was described by the *New York Times* as a "fanciful, lyrical piece about two boys, one Mexican, one white American, and the toy figure of a bandit that the boys make their friend." However, their publisher didn't like it, and the manuscript was lost among Hughes's papers for fifty-seven years. A Hughes scholar tracked it down, and the book was completed at last.

Montmartre, Paris. Hughes wrote about his time in Paris in his first autobiography, *The Big Sea*.

Portrait of the artist as a young man

When it was published, *Publishers Weekly* gave it a glowing review, saying, "The authors focus on such child-pleasing topics as holidays, food and learning to communicate, as the boys teach each other key words in Spanish and English—while gently underscoring the importance of tolerance, self-esteem and sharing."

The Block and *The Sweet and Sour Animal Book* were published **posthumously**. *The Block* uses a series of six collages by African-American artist Romare Bearden as a colorful, vibrant background for Hughes's poems. *The Sweet and Sour Animal Book* contains twenty-six previously unpublished pieces that Hughes wrote in the 1930s, accompanied by illustrations made by elementary-school children at the Harlem School of the Arts. Veronica Chambers, reviewing the finished product in the *New York Times Book Review*, says the poems "reflect Hughes's childlike wonder as well as his sense of humor" and that his poetry offers children "just a simple but seductive taste of the blues."

It's important to note that Hughes never got rich from writing. He seems to have written because he had to—because he enjoyed it, and because he was good at it, certainly, but mostly because it was as much a part of him as his sense of humor or his mustache. He began at a young age and appreciated the praise and attention it brought him, but he also continued to do it almost up until the last days of his life.

CHAPTER FIVE

AN APPRECIATION

Langston Hughes was a lucky writer in that most of what he wrote received critical acclaim, or at least approval. He was especially lucky to be appreciated for his work while he was still alive. When Arthur Spingarn, then-president of the NAACP, presented Hughes with his Spingarn Medal in 1960, he referred to him as "The Poet Laureate of the Negro Race." The Spingarn Medal was just one of many awards and accolades that Hughes won throughout his lifetime, not counting the writing competitions he won earlier in his life.

A CHARMED LIFE

As early as 1925, he won a Guggenheim Fellowship, which, according to the foundation that grants them, "are intended for men and women who have already demonstrated exceptional capacity for

Opposite: German-American artist Winold Reiss drew this portrait of Hughes as part of a series on artists of the Harlem Renaissance.

productive scholarship or exceptional creative ability in the arts." By the ripe old age of twenty-three, Hughes had earned something that the foundation usually grants to midcareer artists. He earned a grant from the American Academy of Arts and Letters, a small, selective honor society of composers, artists, and writers, after being nominated by another member and being approved by a committee. In 1953, he received the Anisfeld-Wolf Award, which "recognize[s] books that have made important contributions to our understanding of racism and human diversity."

Hughes also achieved recognition from the academic community. During his lifetime, he received honorary doctorates in literature from Howard University, Case Western University, and his alma mater, Lincoln University.

The name of Langston Hughes is spoken with such reverence today that it's hard to imagine he was once criticized for some of the things he is now most famous for. For example, Hughes is now praised for his willingness and desire to portray African-American life from all angles—the good, the bad, the ugly, and the beautiful. Some critics, however, didn't appreciate it when he held up the bad or the ugly for examination. One of the few times that Hughes's work created an uproar occurred early in his career.

After the success of his debut poetry collection, *The Weary Blues*, he spent his sophomore year in college working on a second collection, titled *Fine Clothes to the Jew*. While these days it is considered to be Hughes's greatest poetic achievement, it was not well received in its day. Critics of both races, but especially African Americans, disliked the fact that he had written many of the poems in a blues-like vernacular. The white critics couldn't understand why he would do it, and the black critics slammed him, using adjectives like "reeking," "disgusting," "unsanitary," and "repulsive."

Black intellectuals, especially, did not think he should be writing as honestly as he was. Countee Cullen, one of Hughes's Harlem Renaissance peers, had earned an advanced degree at an Ivy League school and had grown up in a very different environment. In reviewing *The Weary Blues* poetry collection for *Opportunity* magazine, he sniffed:

> The selections in this book ... tend to hurl this poet into the gaping pit that lies before all Negro writers, in the confines of which they become racial artists instead of artists pure and simple. There is too much emphasis here on strictly Negro themes; and this is probably an added reason for my coldness toward the jazz poems.

Eustace Gay, the literary critic of the *Philadelphia Tribune*, had a similar reaction to Hughes's second book:

> It does not matter to me whether every poem in the book is true to life. Why should it be paraded before the American public by a Negro author as being typical or representative of the Negro? Bad enough to have white authors holding up our imperfections to public gaze. Our aim ought to be [to] present to the general public, already misinformed both by well meaning and malicious writers, our higher aims and aspirations, and our better selves.

But neither of these dismissals compares to what Hughes himself reported were the critical reactions to *Fine Clothes to the Jew* in his first autobiography, *The Big Sea*:

Countee Cullen

[It] was well received by the literary magazines and the white press, but the Negro critics did not like it at all. The Pittsburgh *Courier* ran a big headline across the top of the page, LANGSTON HUGHES' BOOK OF POEMS TRASH. The headline in the New York *Amsterdam News* was LANGSTON HUGHES—THE SEWER DWELLER. The Chicago *Whip* characterized me as "the poet low-rate of Harlem." Others called the book a disgrace to the race, a return to the dialect tradition, and a parading of all our racial defects before the public … The Negro critics and many of the intellectuals were very sensitive about their race in books. (And still are.) In anything that white people were likely to read, they wanted to put their best foot forward, their politely polished and cultural foot—and only that foot.

In short, the black critics didn't care for his use of dialect or his copying of the rhythms of jazz and blues music—both of which were his trademarks, for which he is now praised—or his focus on poor black people. Hughes's argument was that "polished, educated blacks were not the only blacks worth putting on paper." He later added:

I personally knew very few people anywhere who were wholly beautiful and wholly good … Anyway, I didn't know the upper class Negroes well enough to write much about them. I knew only the people I had grown up with, and they weren't people whose shoes were always shined, who had been to Harvard, or who had heard of Bach. But they seemed to me good people, too.

Even the title stirred up controversy. People were offended, thinking he was being anti-Semitic. Actually, Hughes had named the book after the practice he had seen in poor black communities, where people who desperately needed money would take their clothes to a **pawnbroker** and sell them for cash. Pawnbrokers, in Hughes's experience, tended to be Jewish, and his intent was to highlight the desperation of poor people literally having to sell the clothes off their backs. While it's not unusual for people who have great initial success to undergo a "sophomore slump," Hughes later wondered if the title was too much of a turnoff for potential readers.

Hoyt W. Fuller, a literary critic who later edited *Ebony* magazine and cofounded the Organization of Black American Culture, sided with Hughes, commenting that the writer:

> chose to identify with plain black people—not because it required less effort and sophistication, but precisely because he saw more truth and profound significance in doing so. Perhaps in this he was inversely influenced by his father—who, frustrated by being the object of scorn in his native land, rejected his own people. Perhaps the poet's reaction to his father's flight from the American racial reality drove him to embrace it with extra fervor.

No matter what the professionals thought, Hughes received overwhelming acceptance and love from the average black people that he preferred to write about. As a reviewer for *Black World* said in 1970:

Those whose prerogative it is to determine the rank of writers have never rated him highly, but if the weight of public response is any gauge then Langston Hughes stands at the apex of literary relevance among Black people. The poet occupies such a position in the memory of his people precisely because he recognized that "we possess within ourselves a great reservoir of physical and spiritual strength," and because he used his artistry to reflect this back to the people. He used his poetry and prose to illustrate that "there is no lack within the Negro people of beauty, strength and power," and he chose to do so on their own level, on their own terms.

Perhaps critic and professor David Littlejohn has the last word on the subject. In his book, *Black on White: A Critical Survey of Writing by American Negroes*, he summed up Hughes thusly:

On the whole, Hughes' creative life [was] as full, as varied, and as original as Picasso's, a joyful, honest monument of a career. There [was] no noticeable sham in it, no pretension, no self-deceit; but a great, great deal of delight and smiling irresistible wit. If he seems for the moment upstaged by angrier men, by more complex artists, if "different views engage" us, necessarily, at this trying stage of the race war, he may well outlive them all, and still be there when it's over … Hughes' [greatness] seems to derive from his anonymous unity with his people. He seems to speak for millions, which is a tricky thing to do.

Another area where Hughes fell under the spotlight of harsh criticism was his political beliefs. He made no secret of his interest in socialism and communism. To understand this, consider that he was first introduced to the concept of socialism in high school, when he was young and just beginning to realize that the whole world did not live in segregation and that racism was not an issue in all other countries like it was in the United States. To someone who has nothing, and little hope of owning anything, the idea that all property in a society is public property would be appealing. Also, Hughes believed in equality, and in a socialist society where men and women would have **parity**. He read up on the topic in magazines like the *Liberator,* which published articles by writers like Claude McKay, one of Hughes's favorites.

When he was in his thirties, he started to associate with a communist organization called the John Reed Club, which was mostly made up of artists, writers, and intellectuals who had **left-wing** views of politics and social issues. He started writing for the magazine *New Masses,* which was closely affiliated with the US Communist Party. Hughes stopped short of declaring himself a communist, but he made it clear that he agreed with many of their positions.

This first became a problem when he was staying in Carmel at Noel Sullivan's vacation home. He got involved with the John Reed Club there, lending his presence and his voice to several activities such as a longshoremen's strike. The California media spread the idea that the strikers and their supporters were secretly plotting to overthrow the government. The public started to call for an investigation or arrests. Hughes was singled out for attack—possibly because he was the only black member of the branch—and was forced to leave town much earlier than planned.

Then, in the 1950s, following World War II, anticommunism was running rampant in America. The Cold War between the Soviet Union and the United States made people fearful, even hysterical, over the perceived threat posed by communists in the United States. The leader of the government's investigation into supposed anti-American activities was a senator named Joseph R. McCarthy, who set up the House Un-American Activities Committee in order to root out communists living in America. He went after prominent figures to draw attention to his cause. Since Hughes had been so public about his associations with communist groups and activities, he was called before the committee to be interrogated about his communist sympathies.

Hughes told McCarthy and the rest of the committee that while he once had communist beliefs, he had by and large renounced them. He said he had realized that although the Soviet Union had eliminated racism, he now knew the atrocities they had committed in the name of communism. He assured them that he now knew that communism was not the answer to as many of society's ills as he had once thought.

Hughes was lucky. He didn't end up on the committee's infamous blacklist, which had ruined the careers of many other citizens, especially in the creative arts. He wasn't asked to give names of any friends who he suspected might be communists, as so many other people had had to do. However, he did lose two important friends, who were angry at him for testifying to protect his career: W. E. B. Du Bois and the famous black actor Paul Robeson. He also suffered economic consequences from being called before McCarthy; many spots on an upcoming reading tour were canceled, and some of his remaining events were picketed.

In 1953, Hughes testified before the House Un-American Activities Committee in Washington, DC, to deny that he was a member of the Communist Party.

Anything that impacted Hughes's ability to earn was significant because while Hughes was the first black American to earn his living solely from his writing and public lectures, he never got rich from it. For a good portion of his life, he depended on the generosity of other people, through grants and patronage, to provide him with money to live on. Charlotte Mason and Amy Spingarn gave him money; Noel Sullivan gave him a free place to live when he needed it. One of the drawbacks of being a part of the Harlem Renaissance was that it ended around the time of the Depression, when people couldn't afford to spend money on luxuries like books and theater. Hughes couldn't afford to live on royalties if nobody was buying his books.

One other area where Hughes faced scrutiny and criticism was his sexuality. Although stories exist of Hughes having relationships with women, none of them ever lasted long. He never got married, and he seemed to work hard at projecting an asexual image. Some social critics pan him for this, saying it was a well-known secret that Hughes was gay and that he should have been more open about it, although they admit that self-protection would have been important; he came of age in an era during which gay men—and blacks—were physically and mentally abused for being what they were. Academics and biographers claim that Hughes included hints about his homosexuality in many of his poems, just as Walt Whitman did. They cite Hughes's short story "Blessed Assurance," which deals with a father's anger over his son's effeminacy, among others.

Although Hughes traveled the United States and the rest of the world regularly, he always returned to Harlem, even after the Renaissance ended, many of his friends moved away, and some of the nightclubs shut down. He remained there in the fifties and

POETRY THAT IS MEANT TO BE HEARD

One of the best ways to appreciate Langston Hughes's poetry is to hear it read. Thanks to the Internet, you can hear Hughes himself reading some of his works, or other performers, too. Here are some examples:

www.youtube.com/watch?v=uM7HSOwJw20
Hughes recites his poem "The Weary Blues" (1925) to jazz accompaniment.

www.youtube.com/watch?v=8cKDOGhghMU
Hughes explains the story behind "The Negro Speaks of Rivers" before reading it.

www.youtube.com/watch?v=KyqwvC5s4n8
Here's another reader of "The Weary Blues," accompanied by era-appropriate video and music.

www.youtube.com/watch?v=hz2IOjuxMy0
Hughes reads his poem "Dreams."

www.youtube.com/watch?v=NX9tHuI7zVo
Actress Viola Davis reads "Mother to Son," then Hughes.

www.youtube.com/watch?v=4_6Z1_3btQ8
Hughes reads his poem "Mulatto."

www.youtube.com/watch?v=4CUKyVrhPgM
Hughes shares his thoughts about his poem "I, Too, Sing America" before reciting it.

www.youtube.com/watch?v=HADGKw_wa5E
Actor Danny Glover reads "Ballad of Roosevelt."

Hughes's home on East 127th Street is now on the National Register of Historic Places.

sixties, through the race riots and the drug wars of these decades. Harlem was his home until he died, and even after—his ashes are entombed in the lobby of the Langston Hughes Auditorium at the Schomburg Center for Research in Black Culture, in Harlem.

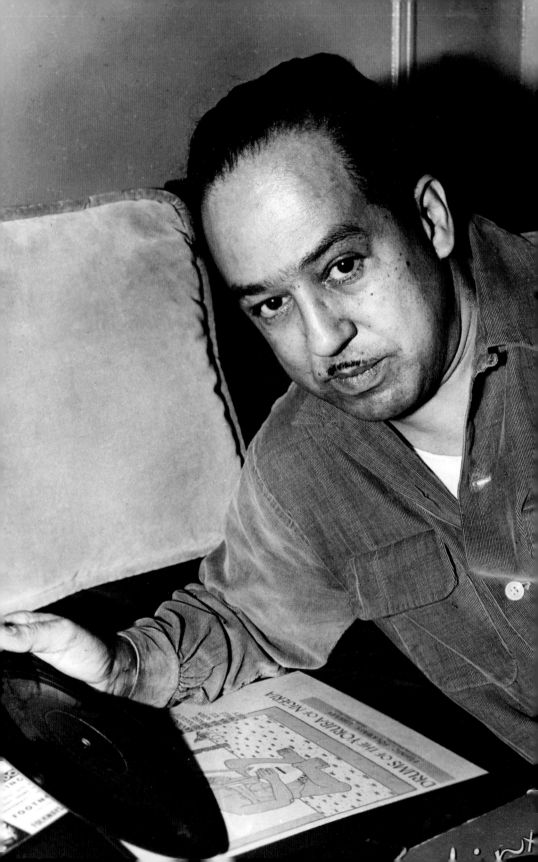

CHAPTER SIX

FIVE DECADES OF WRITING, GENERATIONS OF IMPACT

Anyone who wonders whether Langston Hughes and his works are still considered significant in the twenty-first century need only visit Amazon.com and search his name. Literally thousands of entries come up, on topics ranging from biographies to criticism, fiction to poetry, and African-American studies to history. People write about his life, his work, and his contributions to the fight against racism and for equality. The language he used, the style he embodied, and the trails he blazed are still relevant today.

Students of all ages continue to read and analyze his work. Even the youngest elementary-schoolers can enjoy the sounds of his language and the pictures he painted with words. In fact, picture books are still being created using his poems—one exceptional work illustrates the poem "My People" with sepia photographs of people of color.

Opposite: Hughes at home in 1954

Part of Columbia University's campus, as it looks now

College professors across the country teach whole courses just about Hughes, with names like "Langston Hughes and the Black Aesthetic" and "Langston Hughes: Global Writer" at schools like Columbia, Oberlin and Macalester. There is even a class at Georgia State University linking him to modern culture—"Kanye versus Everybody: Black Poetry and Poetics from Hughes to Hip-Hop"— which makes sense when you consider how Hughes connected the rhythms of music and language. Hughes would probably feel right at home writing in that genre. At the very least, he would probably be thrilled to see the 2015–2016 Broadway sensation *Hamilton*, the musical about founding father Alexander Hamilton, in which almost the entire story is told through today's spoken-word rhymes—rap and hip-hop—by actors and actresses of color.

His impact reaches beyond the classroom and into the culture of performing arts. The City College of New York (CCNY) has been holding an annual Langston Hughes Festival since 1978. CCNY also awards a Langston Hughes Medal each year to recognize an influential and engaging African-American writer. And in his adopted hometown of Lawrence, Kansas, the Department of African and African-American Studies at the University of Kansas (KU) boasts the Langston Hughes Center, which "serves as an academic research and educational center that builds upon the legacy and insight of Langston Hughes." The center has hosted four major symposiums and sponsored nearly eighty academic talks and programs on the topic of Hughes. It also offers programming for the community, such as when the venue was used for a special screening of *Selma*, an Academy Award–nominated film about the life of Martin Luther King Jr., in 2015. In addition to the work of the center, KU supports a Langston Hughes Visiting Professor, who teaches two courses a semester and delivers a campus-wide symposium.

Similarly, Seattle, Washington, is the home of the Langston Hughes Center for the Visual and Performing Arts, a venue that offers performing arts and writing classes for all ages, as well as providing a space to debut plays and musicals and host dance companies and other performances. The center also hosts an annual Langston Hughes African-American Film Festival. The purpose of the nine-day festival is to educate attendees in the art and history of African-American independent film—just as Hughes himself opened the Suitcase Theater to promote the theatrical education of aspiring black writers, directors, actors, and other performing artists.

In Buffalo, New York, the Langston Hughes Institute Center for Cultural History and Arts Education works to develop, preserve, and promote African-American heritage. There are libraries, schools, and community centers named after Langston Hughes throughout the country—including the library at his alma mater, Lincoln University. The tribute that would probably thrill Hughes the most, though, is that the New York Public Library (NYPL) system, which he loved so much, named a building after him. The Langston Hughes Building is part of the NYPL's Schomburg Center for Research in Black Culture, where his ashes were eventually interred.

In 1996, Ron McCurdy, a jazz professor and chair of the African American and African Studies Department at the University of Minnesota, was asked to create a musical work for the opening of the Weisman Art Museum. McCurdy knew right where to look: at an epic poem written by Hughes in 1960 titled *Ask Your Mama: 12 Moods for Jazz*. Hughes had written the poem complete with detailed instructions for musical accompaniment and had planned to perform it with double bassist Charles Mingus, but that collaboration never happened before Hughes's death. Without anything else to go on, McCurdy composed original pieces from Hughes's musical cues and presented the work for the museum's opening. The performance was meant to be a one-time thing, but McCurdy got such an enthusiastic response that he refined and polished the piece and still performs it regularly. He now incorporates video montages showing the historical figures and places anchored in Hughes's poem.

In 2009, Emmy Award–winning composer Laura Karpman had a similar idea. She had stumbled across a copy of *Ask Your Mama* and immediately started to envision it as a multimedia performance. Her version is a spoken-word performance laced with jazz interludes based on Hughes's notes. She incorporated recordings of Hughes reading his own work, along with audio and video of some of the historical figures referenced in the poem such as Leontyne Price, Charlie Parker, and Bo Diddley.

McCurdy's multimedia version of *Ask Your Mama* was performed on a fifty-date tour in 2015. Karpman's version premiered at

Carnegie Hall with opera star Jessye Norman and two members of the hip-hop group the Roots as three of the performers. A later recording, released in 2015, features opera singer Janai Brugger, the Roots, and the San Francisco Ballet Orchestra.

This poem has survived so long and still resonates with modern audiences because of its themes. Hughes wrote the poem after attending the Newport Jazz Festival on a day when riots broke out—and now riots break out in the United States regularly, sparked by the deaths of young African-American men at the hands of police. It's amazing but sad that the same social issues being argued today are the ones that Langston Hughes was writing about fifty years ago.

Hughes's racial consciousness and pride, as well as his depictions of black life, have influenced several generations of artists and activists in the United States, Africa and even the Caribbean. Writers like Puerto Rican poet and professor Martín Espada, African-Latin American author Manuel Zapata Olivella, and spoken-word performer Gil Scott-Heron (who was also a "jazz poet" and a novelist) have all cited Hughes as an influence on their writing. Olivella's **prodigious** correspondence with Hughes was written about in the *Afro-Hispanic Review*, and the essay's author, Laurence Prescott, may as well have been writing about Hughes himself when he described Olivella:

> Unlike many of his contemporaries, Zapata Olivella unapologetically places Black Latin Americans, mulattoes, and the marginalized poor in the center of his narrations in order to give voice and representation to the dispossessed, while rendering social critique.

Hughes was friends with, and gave constant encouragement to, younger African-American poets, such as Mari Evans. He and Evans became friends after he included her work in 1964's *New Negro Poets: USA*. Caribbean-American writer, poet, and activist Audre Lorde had a similar introduction to Hughes, through his selection of her work for another anthology he was editing. Hughes also supported poets Sarah Webster Fabio, Ishmael Reed, and Raymond Patterson—who later became the founder of New York City College's Langston Hughes Festival. Reed introduced Hughes to the poetry of Lucille Clifton, who later became poet laureate of Maryland and was nominated twice for the Pulitzer Prize for poetry.

On a more personal level, there are those writers and performers who give direct credit to Hughes for influencing their work and their lives. Alice Walker is probably the most famous of his protégés, having won the Pulitzer Prize for her third novel, *The Color Purple*, which was also turned into a movie and a Broadway musical.

As a senior at Sarah Lawrence College in New York City, Walker already had support and encouragement in her writing from poets Muriel Ruykeyser and Jane Cooper. After an intense stint of depression and anxiety following an abortion, a decision she had agonized over for weeks, she turned to fiction and pounded out a short story called "To Hell with Dying." Ruykeyser sent the story to publishers as well as to Hughes. Not only did Walker receive a handwritten note of encouragement from Hughes, but he included the story in an anthology he was editing, called *The Best Short Stories By Negro Writers: An Anthology from 1899 to the Present*. As if that weren't enough, he mentioned Walker's story specifically in the introduction he wrote, saying

"Neither you nor I have read a story like hers before. At least, I don't think you have."

Hughes said he was struck by Walker's lyrical language and the story's affirmation of the same type of values he'd always cherished. He later bragged to his longtime friend Arna Bontemps, "Mine is her first important publication (and her first story in print), so I can claim her discovery, too, I reckon." Meanwhile, twenty years later, Walker remembered the episode with wonder, saying, "[He] published my first short story, and his support of me in other ways meant more to me than I can say." She added:

> "Who was this man? … That he should care so much about a young and unknown writer? That he should write to me; that he would take for granted that yes, of course, I was a writer and should be respected as one. How could he be so kind, so generous?"

Playwright Loften Mitchell, a generation younger than Hughes, published a piece in a 1968 issue of *Black World/Negro Digest* called "An Informal Memoir: For Langston Hughes and Stella Holt." In it, he told of meeting Hughes as a child in Harlem, through a group for young actors, when he attended a performance of *Don't You Want to Be Free?* Years later, as an associate producer for a theater company, he met Hughes again when the older playwright attended a performance. The two began running into each other at theatrical events and always ended up talking about writing, Mitchell said. He recounted a story about Hughes being happy for him when his show got produced at a certain theater instead of *Simply Heavenly*, as had been planned, and called Hughes "a big, big man with a big, big heart."

OTHER TRIBUTES

Langston Hughes is still very much a part of life in New York City. His home on East 127th Street in Harlem, a brownstone rowhouse that he inhabited for the last twenty years of his life, is the place where he lived the longest and is the most tangible symbol of his association with Harlem. It has been on the National Register of Historic Places since 1982, and the street was officially renamed "Langston Hughes Place."

Officials in the town of Lawrence, Kansas, are making plans to honor Hughes with a statue in his likeness, to be placed in Watson Park, a few blocks from where he lived with his grandmother.

In 2002, the United States Postal Service honored Hughes with a commemorative stamp bearing his image. It was the twenty-fifth stamp in their Black Heritage series.

Hughes was honored by the US Postal Service in 2002 with a stamp bearing his likeness.

"He had been out there alone for many, many years … he created an atmosphere, a climate, among black writers—a brotherhood," Mitchell wrote. Another time, he said, "Langston set a tone, a standard of brotherhood and friendship and cooperation,

Author Alice Walker.

for all of us to follow. You never got from him, 'I am the Negro writer,' but only 'I am a Negro writer.' He never stopped thinking about the rest of us." Mitchell, who kept writing plays and stayed involved in theater after Hughes's death, went on to be nominated for a Tony Award in 1976.

Then there is novelist Paule Marshall, who devoted the opening chapter in her autobiography *Triangular Road* to Hughes—the title of the chapter is "Homage to Mr. Hughes," in which she tells the story of an overseas trip she took with Hughes in 1965, when she was in her mid-thirties Hughes chose her to accompany him on the tour, during which they both read their work, which was a tremendous boost for her career. She described him as "an **avuncular**, generous man who talked freely with [me] about literature, life and black American culture and history." She called him "a loving taskmaster, mentor, teacher, **griot**, literary sponsor and treasured elder friend," and added, "Decades have passed since his death in 1967 and I still miss him."

Langston Hughes was an innovator. In his poetry, in addition to making free verse accessible, he used music, rhythm, and images that professed his African-American literary heritage. He incorporated the styles of jazz and blues for the structure and subjects of his poems. Whether he was writing poetry or prose, musicals or magazine articles, he wrote about everyone in black society, with a focus on the common man and his everyday struggles. He wanted to uplift the condition of his people, raise racial consciousness and cultural nationalism, and shout to the rooftops that they should have pride in their diversity. Perhaps because equality has not been achieved, and racism still exists in America, his work still resonates today.

CHRONOLOGY

1902 Born on February 1 in Joplin, Missouri, to James and Carolina (Carrie) Hughes.

1909 Moves to Lawrence, Kansas, to live with his grandmother, Mary Langston.

1915 Lives with family friends for two years after Mary Langston dies.

1916 Moves to Chicago, then Cleveland, to live with his mother, her second husband, and his half-brother.

1917 Lives in Cleveland on his own after his mother moves back to Chicago so he can finish high school where he started.

1919 Spends the summer in Mexico with his father.

1920 Graduates from Central High School in Cleveland, Ohio.

1921 Publishes the poem "The Negro Speaks of Rivers" and enrolls at Columbia University with plans to become a writer.

1922 Quits school and begins taking odd jobs so he can meet new people and travel the world.

1924 Returns to the United States.

1926 Publishes his first book, *The Weary Blues*, and enrolls at Lincoln University.

1929 Graduates from Lincoln University.

1932 Travels to the Soviet Union and Asia.

1934 Publishes his first book of short stories, *The Ways of White Folks*; his father dies.

1937 Covers the Spanish Civil War for the *Afro-American*.

1938 Founds Suitcase Theater in Harlem with friend Louise Thompson.

1953 Testifies before Senator Joseph McCarthy's Senate Permanent Subcommittee on Investigations.

1960 Receives the Spingarn Medal.

1961 Inducted into the National Institute of Arts and Letters.

1967 Passes away on May 22 in New York City.

HUGHES'S MOST IMPORTANT WORKS

POETRY COLLECTIONS

The Weary Blues (1926)
Fine Clothes to the Jew (1927)
The Negro Mother and Other Dramatic Recitations (1931)
Dear Lovely Death (1931)
The Dream Keeper and Other Poems (1932)
Shakespeare in Harlem (1942)
Freedom's Plow (1943)
Montage of a Dream Deferred (1951)
Ask Your Mama: 12 Moods for Jazz (1961)
The Panther and the Lash: Poems of Our Times (1967)

SHORT STORY COLLECTIONS/FICTION

Not Without Laughter (1930)
The Ways of White Folks (1934)
Simple Speaks His Mind (1950)
Simple Takes a Wife (1953)
Simple Stakes a Claim (1957)
Tambourines to Glory (1958)
The Best of Simple (1961)
Something in Common and Other Stories (1963)
Simple's Uncle Sam (1965)

NON-FICTION

The Big Sea (1940)
Famous American Negroes (1954)
I Wonder as I Wander (1956)
Famous Negro Heroes of America (1958)
Fight for Freedom: The Story of the NAACP (1962)

MAJOR PLAYS

Mulatto (1935)
Little Ham (1936)
Don't You Want to Be Free? (1938)
Tambourines to Glory (1956)
Simply Heavenly (1957)
Black Nativity (1961)
Jericho-Jim Crow (1964)

WORKS FOR CHILDREN

Popo and Fifina, with Arna Bontemps (1932)
The Pasteboard Bandit, with Arna Bontemps
    (written 1935, published 1997)
The First Book of the Negroes (1952)
The First Book of Jazz (1954)
The First Book of Rhythms (1954)
The First Book of the West Indies (1956)
The First Book of Africa (1964)

GLOSSARY

advance Payment beforehand, especially when an author receives money in advance of the publication of his or her book.

arsenal An establishment normally operated by the government to store and issue arms or other military equipment.

avuncular Acting or speaking with the familiarity or kindness of an uncle.

bar exam A test administered in each state to assess whether or not a candidate is competent to practice law in that jurisdiction.

epicenter The central point of something.

grant A gift of money usually given by an organization or government for a particular purpose.

griot West-African musician-entertainers or storytellers whose performances include tribal histories and genealogies.

idyllic Something that is pleasing or picturesque.

Jim Crow laws State and local laws enforcing racial segregation in the Southern United States.

leftist Someone who supports liberal political positions or activities that accept or support social equality.

left-wing The radically liberal members of a political group.

Marxism The theory of Karl Marx which says that society's classes are the cause of political struggle and that social classes should be eliminated.

militant Given to fighting.

onomatopoeia The formation of words in imitation of natural sounds.

ostensible Appearing to be true, although not necessarily so.

parity The quality or state of being equal.

pawnbroker Someone who loans money on the security of personal property pledged in his keeping.

posthumous Following or occurring after one's death.

prodigious Extraordinary in bulk, extent, quantity, or degree.

propaganda Dissemination of ideas, information, or rumor for the purpose of helping or injuring an institution, a cause, or a person.

rhapsodize To speak or write about someone or something with great enthusiasm.

socialism Social and political movements advocating collective or governmental ownership and administration of the means of production.

solace Comfort in grief.

stipend A regular allowance paid to help with living expenses.

travelogue A talk, lecture, or book about the places visited by a traveler.

vernacular Using a language or dialect native to a region or country rather than a literary language.

BOOKS

Leach, Laurie. *Langston Hughes: A Biography.* Westport, CT: Greenwood Press, 2004.

Meltzer, Milton. *Langston Hughes: An Illustrated Edition.* Brookfield, CT: The Millbrook Press, 1997.

Osofsky, Audrey. *Free to Dream: The Making of a Poet, Langston Hughes.* New York: Lothrop, Lee & Shepard, 1996.

AUDIO/VIDEO

Jessye Norman, the Roots Team Up for Langston Hughes' 'Ask Your Mama'
www.pbs.org/newshour/art/jessye-norman-the-roots-team-up-for-langston-hughes-ask-your-mama
Audio clips from Laura Karpman's show can be heard here.

The Langston Hughes Project
langstonhughesproject.org
A trailer for Ron McCurdy's show and an audio recording of one entire performance can be seen and heard here.

WEBSITES

Langston Hughes—A Few Harlem Stops on His Birthday

www.boweryboyshistory.com/2012/02/langston-hughes-few-harlem-stops-on-his.html

This site shows you where and how to follow in the footsteps of Langston Hughes through Harlem and visit his final resting place.

Langston Hughes – Biography

www.biography.com/people/langston-hughes-9346313#video-gallery

Facts, photos, and videos highlight this entry about one of America's leading poets.

Must-See Harlem

www.nycgo.com/articles/must-see-harlem

Use this site to guide you through modern-day Harlem and its historical sites.

PBS Masterpiece: Langston Hughes

www.pbs.org/wgbh/masterpiece/americancollection/cora/ei_hughesbiography.html

This site features essays and interviews, a timeline about Hughes's life, information about the Harlem Renaissance, and some of his works.

PoemHunter: Langston Hughes

www.poemhunter.com/langston-hughes

Access more than one hundred of Hughes's poems here.

BIBLIOGRAPHY

Als, Hilton. "The Sojourner: The Elusive Langston Hughes." *New Yorker*, February 23 and March 2, 2015. http://www.newyorker.com/magazine/2015/02/23/sojourner.

Haugen, Brenda. *Langston Hughes: The Voice of Harlem*. Minneapolis, MN: Compass Point Books, 2006.

Hill, Christine M. *Langston Hughes: Poet of the Harlem Renaissance*. Springfield, NJ: Enslow Publishers, 1997.

"Langston Hughes." Poets.org. https://www.poets.org/poetsorg/poet/langston-hughes.

"Langston Hughes, Writer, 65, Dead." *New York Times*, May 23, 1967. http://www.nytimes.com/learning/general/onthisday/bday/0201.html.

Life of Langston Hughes, The (blog). http://lifeoflangstonhughes.blogspot.com.

McKissack, Patricia, and Fredrick McKissack. *Langston Hughes: Great American Poet.* Revised Edition. Springfield, NJ: Enslow Publishers, 2002.

Raatma, Lucia. *Langston Hughes: African-American Poet*. Chanhassen, MN: The Child's World, 2003.

Rampersad, Arnold. "Hughes's Life and Career." Modern American Poetry. http://www.english.illinois.edu/maps/poets/g_l/hughes/life.htm.

Rummel, Jack. *Langston Hughes, Poet*. Black Americans of Achievement. New York: Chelsea House, 1988.

Walker, Alice. *Langston Hughes, American Poet*. New York: HarperCollins Publishers, 2002.

INDEX

Page numbers in **boldface** are illustrations. Entries in **boldface** are glossary terms.

advance, 55
arsenal, 9–10
avuncular, 115

bar exam, 8
Bethune, Mary McLeod, 50–51, **52**, 53
Bontemps, Arna, 39, 53, 61, 67, 78, 86, 111
Brown, John, 9–11

Calloway, Cab, 44, **45**
Columbia University, 21, 23, 25, 27, 29–30, **31**, **106**
Cullen, Countee, 30, 38, 41, 63, 78–79, 93, **94**

epicenter, 8, 25

grant, 51, 91–92, 101
griot, 115

Hughes, Langston
  awards, 41, 43, 49, 53, 66, 81, 91–92
  children's books, 53, 55, 78, 86, 89
  critical reception, 43, 55, 57, 59, 61, 83, 85, 89, 92–93, 95–97, 101
  drama, 47, 59, 61, 65, 77, 80, **81**, 111
  early life, 7–9, 11, 13, **14**, 15–16, **17**, 18–19, 21–23, 25
  fiction, 47, 49, **56**, 57, 65, 80–83, **84**, 85, 101
  legacy, 7, 105–112, **113**, 114–115
  nonfiction, 57, 60–62, **64**, 65–66, 85–86, **87**
  poetry, 18, 21–23, 30, 35, 37–39, 41, 43, 47, 50–51, 57, 59, 61–62, 64, **66**, 67, 72–77, 102, 108–109
  race and, 8, 13, 15, 18, 27, 29, 32–34, 38, 44, 51,

53, 55, 71–77, 109
style, 35, 50, 62–63, 73–75, 77, 92, 95, 106
travels, 19, 21–23, 32–35, 37–38, 49–51, 53–55, 58–61, 65, 85–86, **87**, 115
Hurston, Zora Neale, 41, 47, 80, **81**

idyllic, 58
"I, Too, Sing America," 38, 62, 75–76

Jim Crow laws, 8, 34, 75–76, 83
Johnson, Charles S., 38–39, 41, **48**

leftist, 57
left-wing, 98
Lindsay, Vachel, 39, 41, 73
Lincoln University, 43–44, 47, 49, 81, 92, 107

Marshall, Thurgood, 44
Marxism, 57
Mason, Charlotte Osgood, **46**, 47, 50, 81, 101
militant, 10
Montage of a Dream Deferred, 35, 37, 64, 74–75

"Negro Speaks of Rivers, The," 21–23, 67, 73

onomatopoeia, 35
ostensible, 54

parity, 98
pawnbroker, 96
Popo and Fifina, 53, 55, 86
posthumous, 89
prodigious, 109
propaganda, 57

rhapsodize, 15

Simple stories, 65, 82–83, **84**, 85
socialism, 54–55, 57, 72, 98
solace, 16
stipend, 47

travelogue, 65

vernacular, 80, 92

Walker, Alice, 71, 110–111, **114**
Weary Blues, The, 41, 73, 92–93
Whitman, Walt, 62, **63**, 75, 101

ABOUT THE AUTHOR

Rebecca Carey Rohan lives in upstate New York with her two children and three rescued pets. She is the author of *Working with Electricity: Electrical Engineers, Great American Thinkers: Thurgood Marshall*, and two other titles in the Artists of the Harlem Renaissance series, *Duke Ellington* and *Billie Holiday*.